LETCHWORTH SETTLEMENT
1920–2020

A century of creative learning

Kate Thompson

HERTFORDSHIRE PUBLICATIONS
an imprint of
University of Hertfordshire Press

First published in Great Britain in 2020 by
Hertfordshire Publications
an imprint of
University of Hertfordshire Press
College Lane
Hatfield
Hertfordshire
AL10 9AB

The right of Kate Thompson to be identified as the author of this work has been asserted by her in accordance with the Copyright, Designs and Patents Act 1988.

British Library Cataloguing in Publication Data
A catalogue record for this book is available from the British Library

ISBN 978-1-912260-29-4

Design by Arthouse Publishing Solutions
Printed in Great Britain by Hobbs the Printers Ltd

CONTENTS

Publication has been generously supported by the following subscribers:

Mark & Marion Adams
Val Aitken
Michael Andrews
Jacqueline Angell
Catherine Antrobus
M C Baffoni
Clare Bandy
Elizabeth Barber
Val Barber
Dr E B Barron
Laurence D G Barwell
Pat Baskerville
Sue & Peter Bathmaker
Peter Belton
John & Roberta Bird
Teena Blackmore
Derek Blyth
Carole Brooks
Annie Burcombe
Pam & Bob Burn
Anthony Burrows
Yvonne Cadwallader
Nigel & Sarah Carrick
Ken Chapman
Peter & Francoise Chapman
Stephen Charles
John Collins
Mary Cox
Sally Day
Bernard Drummond
Kathleen Elson
Jeremy Evans
Roy Evans

Schreuder Family
Sheila Farey
Margaret Fitzpatrick
Carola & David Garvie
Jackie Gough
John Hall
Anne Hassall
Pamela Haynes
Wendy Heaney
Barbara Heaton
Graham Holley
Hilary & Tony Howell
Maggie & Tony James
Chris Jones
Fran Kelly
Pat & Leslie Large
Paula Lawrence
Peter Lee
Robin Lipscombe
Allan Lupton
Katie Maynard-Smith
Roger & Liz Mcintyre-Brown
Susan Mellor
Michelle Metz
Freddie Morris
Mo & Ian Mutton
Judith & Peter Nash
Barry Neale
K W Needham
Charlie & Richard Nunn
Mary Penny
Stephen Pike
Sue Pike

Paul & Gill Pritchard
Rosemary & Tony Read
Sheila Rhodes
Tracy Rudeforth
Raymond Scroggins
Derek Searle
Mildred Sharman
Pauline Shepherd
Chris Snoad
Maureen Sparkes
Gloria Spicer
Peter & Angela Spreckley
Frances Spurrier
Robert Staddon
Helen Taylor
Valerie Thorning
Bob & Margaret Thorogood
Roger Thorp
Michael & Lesley Thurman
David Tinney
Janice Trollope
Jan & Tricia Turner
Anne-Marie Wadood
Dianne Wallace
Margaret Warren
Michael Warren
Ella & John Webb
Mrs A M West
Sonia & Rick Weston
Sandra & David Wilkins
Alison Wormleighton
Barbara Young

The Settlement Management Committee at the time the book was published were:

President: John Bird   Peter Chapman
Chair: Pam Burn   Elizabeth Barber
Vice Chair: Barry Neale   Bob Thorogood
Secretary: Tony James   Sue Pike

Manager: Sonia Weston
Deputy Manager: Sally Rogers
Press and PR: Rachel Lawrence-Hyde

ACKNOWLEDGEMENTS

P am Burn pays tribute to the team who helped with this book in her Foreword. Any errors are mine alone. I would like to thank Jane Housham and her team at Hertfordshire Publications for their tremendous support and enthusiasm for the project. Aimee and Sophie at the Garden City Collection were very generous with their time and scanned many of the images in the book. Ros Allwood of North Hertfordshire Museum drew my attention to the Elsie Lamb painting. Tony James photographed items that are not in the Garden City Collection, and enhanced many of the photographs from newspapers reproduced in these pages (which are often the only record of an event).

Inga Horwood and Thogdin Ripley kindly allowed me to quote from the histories of the Settlement Players, in the latter case on behalf of his late grandfather, Noel Ripley.

When Pam first approached me, I felt the project was a worthwhile one and, if anything, the research I did increased this view. I hope you enjoy reading it.

Kate Thompson
Letchworth Garden City
March 2020

ILLUSTRATIONS

Unless credited otherwise, all illustrations are taken from the Settlement's archive, held either at the Garden City Collection (GCC) or in the Nevells Road building itself.

Figures

Colour plates

FOREWORD

When I was elected Chair of Letchworth Settlement at the end of 2014, I spent quite a bit of time researching our Settlement and other Settlements here and in the USA. I found lots of papers, leaflets, mentions in other documents but – to my astonishment – no books, other than one or two written long ago for Toynbee Hall in London, the first Settlement House.

Over the years since, the idea of a book stayed with me and, in preparation for our centenary year in 2020, I determined that there had to be A Book! At first I thought I would write it myself – something I had always wanted to do. However, commitments to other organisations took more and more of my time and it became clear that I could not deliver this book personally.

It was my husband who suggested I ask Kate Thompson for help. They both belonged to a walking group and when he mentioned her to me, I realised that she and I had both worked at Herts County Council back in the early 1990s. I invited her round for coffee and a chat and the rest, as they say, is history! Kate, who has written several other books and is a noted speaker on many subjects, 'allowed' me to twist her arm and within a short period of time she had gathered a small group of willing researchers to tackle the mound of documents which had been gifted to the Letchworth Garden City Heritage Foundation archives in 2015 under the, perhaps optimistic, name of 'the Settlement Archive'.

I was astonished at what Ellen Barnes was able to produce in terms of research notes when I first met up with her and Kate to discuss progress in the autumn of 2019. At last it seemed my book just *might* become a reality! Kate made contact with Dr Mark Freeman of UCL whom I had met in early 2015 when I was first looking at the archives and he gave us good advice and has kindly written the Preface to this book. Roy Evans, the last Warden of the Settlement and still much involved today, gave Kate dates, names and explanations when the paperwork gave none. Sue Bathmaker, Aimee Flack, Sophie Walter, Sarah and Nigel Carrick, and Sonia Weston helped Ellen with the research, Philippa Parker with proof-reading, Tony James with photos and illustrations and I read the chapters and made a few suggestions which Kate *sometimes* accepted! Finally, Vanessa Stone, paper-cutting and collage artist with strong connections to Letchworth and the Settlement itself having run many workshops there, kindly allowed us to use one of her striking pieces for the front cover of the book.

The Settlement and I owe Kate and this small team of people she gathered around her a huge debt of gratitude. I read every chapter with increasing fascination – all those people attending all those courses – who would have thought that fifty-one people would attend a class on Economics in 1930? Or that George Bernard Shaw or E M Forster would have come along to a meeting?

There is much more to learn about the life and times of our predecessors here in the world's First Garden City of Letchworth, the guiding principles of which included a healthy mind as well as a healthy body. To my mind, it is no accident that the Settlement remains here in this town, still vibrant and active, still trying to find new things to teach and share with people who are still keen to meet, to learn and to create. Here's to the next 100 years!

Pam Burn
Chair
March 2020

P.S. The coronavirus pandemic which struck the world in early 2020 caused the Settlement to close its doors to students as the country went into 'lockdown'. As we go to press at the end of June 2020, the Settlement is running a major fundraising campaign to enable it to restart all its operations later in 2020 or early in 2021. The Hall and theatre will be opened as soon as government conditions allow. Our campaign is proving to be very successful and offers of help are coming in from many quarters. Government regulations are being eased. A new Management Committee is being formed to take on the challenge of restarting all our activities gradually over the months to come. Subject to there being no second wave of the virus, I am confident that, at this point in time, the Settlement will survive once again. The work to deliver creative learning goes on.

PREFACE

I t was an honour to be asked by Pam Burn and Kate Thompson to write the preface to this centenary history of the Letchworth Settlement. It is a story that deserves to be more widely known among historians and educationalists, and in the town of Letchworth and beyond. I have seen the archival material held at the Settlement, and have spent many hours myself working through the archives of the Educational Centres Association (ECA) in London. To distil this considerable quantity of material into a meaningful and accessible account is no mean achievement, and Kate should be congratulated for it. Letchworth Settlement has many unique features, but it has also been part of a bigger story of adult education across the past century, and as such this book should be of interest both locally and to others interested in the history of adult learning.

What strikes me most on reading *Letchworth Settlement, 1920–2020* is the sheer range and variety of educational experiences that learners have enjoyed in Letchworth over the past century. From the start, courses on economics and industrial history run by the Workers' Educational Association (WEA) shared the premises with art and music appreciation, folk dancing, book groups, language classes, popular science lectures and – as time went on – English for speakers of other languages. And this is not to mention the huge range of social and informal educational activities, many of which are detailed in chapter 8: drama has been an important feature since the 1920s, while other interests – in photography, music and rambling, for example – have waxed and waned. Like other educational institutions, the Letchworth Settlement moved with the times. Kate notes the rise and fall of Esperanto, the interwar enthusiasm for 'Regional Survey', the importance of sewing and crafts during the second world war, and the existence of courses on industrial sociology in the early 1960s. There was even a special class to prepare housewives for decimalisation in 1971 (see chapter 6). Well-known speakers have visited the Settlement, ranging from the former Secretary of State for War, Viscount Haldane, in 1921, to E M Forster in 1930, to the Armitage lecturers – including Shirley Williams, Jo Grimond, Baroness Warnock and Terry Waite – in the 1980s and 1990s. Meanwhile, local history, it seems, has always been popular in and around Letchworth, and has remained a staple of the Settlement's activities.

Many themes identified in Kate's book recur across the wider history of adult education in modern Britain. The importance of international educational travel, the sometimes uneasy co-existence of university-level education and popular 'recreational' courses, and the repeated worries about funding are all important examples. The difficulties of retaining Settlement wardens at Letchworth in the 1940s and 1950s were reflected across an adult education sector that was anxious about its status and unable to pay its staff well. In other ways Letchworth was unusual, or even pioneering, most notably perhaps in the Settlement's work in the villages, of which Mary Ibberson's music classes, described in chapter 4, were a particularly important example.

At various points in the book, we see the shadow of the Ministry of Reconstruction report on adult education, published in 1919. This is often seen as a key statement of the value of 'liberal' adult education, and championed the role of voluntary providers such as the WEA. The emergence of educational settlements like the one at Letchworth – and, in 1919–20, the ECA – was another important aspect of this early post-war climate of growth and optimism. The subsequent century has seen an evolving relationship between voluntary providers and the state, as well as ups and – perhaps more frequently – downs in the funding and status of the kind of adult learning that has been fostered at the Letchworth Settlement. In 2019 the current prospects were set out by the Centenary Commission on Adult Education, a group inspired by the example of the 1919 report. Chaired by Dame Helen Ghosh, the Master of Balliol, the Centenary Commission powerfully restated the view of its predecessor in 1919 that adult education is, and will remain, a 'permanent national necessity', and further argued that this necessity is especially urgent in today's context of 'a fractured society and democracy', in which the 'promotion of community cohesion' is a key political challenge. Local adult education institutions have their role to play in this, and this includes the Letchworth Settlement.

Like the members of last year's Centenary Commission, the management committee of the Letchworth Settlement are motivated by a desire to understand and learn from the past, and hence they too have commissioned a publication – in this case, Kate's fascinating and valuable historical account of the Settlement and its varied work during the past hundred years. In chapter 3, Kate quotes the post-war Settlement warden, Cedric Davies, who in 1948 lamented a tendency 'to decry or forget all that has been done in the past'. This book will ensure that the history of the Settlement will be neither decried nor forgotten. It resurrects an important history and makes it accessible – and, I think, inspiring – for those who come to the Settlement in the future.

Mark Freeman
Reader in Education and Social History
Institute of Education, University College London

Chapter 1

THE SETTLEMENT MOVEMENT

The Letchworth Adult Educational Settlement, to give it its full title, held an inaugural public meeting on 8 May 1920, sponsored by Dr Ralph Crowley of the Board of Education. It was part of a wider movement intended to help working men and women who would otherwise have little or no access to education, and built on the earlier adult school movement, which began in the late 1790s and was a significant element in the provision of adult education in Britain. The term 'Settlement' was coined by Rev Samuel Barnett (see p. 2).

The adult school movement can be seen as the forerunner to settlements; it started as a way to teach adults to read the Bible and was linked with the Society for Promoting Christian Knowledge (SPCK), established by the Church of England.[1] The first adult school is believed to have begun in Nottingham in 1798 to meet the needs of younger women workers in lace and hosiery factories. Adult schools were founded in Southwark in 1814 and in the City of London the following year. They met on Sundays and from the middle of the nineteenth century subjects other than reading were taught. By the end of the century there were about 350 schools and about 45,000 students. A National Council of Adult Schools was formed in 1899 to federate existing associations and promote their work. There was a rapid growth in participation in the years leading up to the first world war; by 1909–10, at its peak, there were about 1,900 schools and nearly 114,000 adult learners. This marked the high point of the adult school movement and numbers declined quite dramatically thereafter. Interestingly, men's membership fell much faster than women's. The reasons for this decline are discussed by Mark Freeman, one of the leading historians of the adult school movement.[2] Competition from more secular organisations played a part and Freeman identified three other reasons: they represented an outdated form of social patronage; their leaders were getting older and younger people were not being recruited; and there was a lack of clear-cut aims. He quotes a scathing verdict from 1938 by W E Williams, secretary of the British

Institute of Adult Education, who characterised adult schools as 'a movement which has fallen between two stools of evangelism and education and which for all its merits is as incapable of surviving the pressure of modern educational needs as the magic lantern is of competing against the cinema'.[3]

The inter-war years were difficult for adult schools, as described by Freeman.[4] He argues that they pursued a strategy of 'resistance' to secularisation, and increasingly concentrated on their core religious activities rather than trying to compete with other adult education providers. By the 1930s the student body was largely made up of older men and women. The movement faced competition from the Workers' Educational Association (WEA), founded in 1903, and university extension classes. The number of WEA students rose from 12,000 in 1920 to 67,000 at the outbreak of the second world war.[5]

Adult schools and educational settlements were very different but, because there were few settlements in certain parts of the country, adult schools continued to exist there. Nevertheless, some of the problems felt by the adult school movement were later replicated in settlements.

The settlement movement is generally thought to have originated with Toynbee Hall in east London, building on the work of the Charity Organisation Society, formed in 1869. Toynbee Hall was created in 1884 by Samuel and Henrietta Barnett; Samuel was the vicar of St Jude's church in Whitechapel and Henrietta a teacher, philanthropist and social activist. The idea apparently arose after Samuel Barnett visited his friend, the economic historian Arnold Toynbee, in Oxford in 1875.[6] Toynbee graduated in 1878 and then taught at his college, Balliol College Oxford. He was actively involved in improving the living conditions of the working poor, based in Whitechapel, where he helped to establish public libraries aimed at assisting working-class men and women. He also encouraged his students to offer free courses for the working class in their own neighbourhoods.[7] Both Toynbee and Barnett inspired other students to become part of their vision to improve other people's lives.

Samuel and Henrietta Barnett began by offering evening classes to adults with music and other entertainment, but their ambition was to provide a designated house where people could come together as a community.[8] In his book *Practicable Socialism: Essays on Social Reform* (1888), Samuel said: 'A Settlement is simply a means by which men and women may share themselves with their neighbours; a club-house in an industrial district, where the condition of membership is the performance of a citizen's duty; a house among the poor, where residents may make friends with the poor.'[9] They established Toynbee Hall in response to a growing realisation that enduring social change would not be achieved through the existing individualised and piecemeal approaches. The radical vision was to create a place for future leaders to live and work as volunteers in London's East End, bringing them face to face with poverty, and giving them the opportunity to develop practical solutions that they could take with them into national life. It was named after their friend who had died in 1883, aged only thirty.[10] Many of the individuals who came to Toynbee Hall as young men and women – including Clement Attlee and William Beveridge – went on to bring about radical social change and maintained a lifelong connection with the institution.[11] Toynbee Hall is still active today.

Other settlements followed, not just in the UK; as early as 1886, a number were founded in the USA, and there were others in Europe, Japan and Australia.[12] The British movement was particularly strong in the north of England where the early settlements grew from Quaker adult schools. The Rowntree family of York were probably the most important pioneers and were closely associated with the first two settlements, in Leeds and York, which were non-residential. The Swarthmore Settlement in Leeds was founded by Quakers in 1909 and is still in existence; two Quakers are on its Council.[13] St Mary's Educational Settlement in York was also founded in 1909 but appears to have ended in 1976; fortunately, its archives have been preserved.[14] Two of the early settlements were residential – Woodbrooke and Fircroft, both in Birmingham, created in 1903 and 1909 respectively.[15]

The Joseph Rowntree Charitable Trust, established in 1904, became the main financial supporter of the educational settlement movement in the inter-war years.[16] Other settlements followed, largely after the first world war; most of them, like Letchworth, were non-residential. The Educational Settlements Association (ESA) was formed in 1920 and by 1935 had thirty-two member settlements, including Letchworth. In 1924 it became entitled to statutory financial support for the provision of adult education; from this date the Rowntree Trust also decided that the bulk of its adult-education funding would go to the ESA.

A pamphlet entitled 'What is an Educational Settlement?' is held in the Settlement archives. It dates from February 1927 and refers to twelve settlements, including Letchworth, of which five were residential. It begins by setting out the rationale behind the settlement movement:

> An Educational Settlement is a centre in which men and women gather to pursue knowledge and wisdom in harmonising fellowship; it is also a centre of co-operation and social life for all the agencies for adult education in the neighbourhood, while it organises co-operatively work which such agencies separately neither wish nor are able to undertake.[17]

It discusses the subjects taught and describes some of the institutions, as well as the 'pioneer work' in rural areas. It contains quotations from the Archbishop of York, Lord Haldane, the Duchess of Atholl and Miss Margaret Bondfield, MP. The last said:

The Settlements of which I have personal knowledge have always seemed to me to be of great value in focussing attention upon the importance of developing personality, and of encouraging in the workers those talents that are usually rendered abortive by the struggle for bread. Between the quiet garden and the Community Play there is a whole range of activities to suit all ages and temperaments.[18]

There were also comments from three users: a factory girl, an agricultural worker and a student. The factory girl said:

For a whole year I really lived and, furthermore, I learned to appreciate most of the things that make life worthwhile. I returned to the old life but the old life had disappeared. I arrived home to find everything different… Buildings which had stood for years almost unnoticed by me suddenly became interesting.[19]

Educational settlements were involved in helping to relieve distress. A settlement in the Welsh coalfields provided a soup kitchen as well as classes aimed at improving the long-term welfare and prospects of the unemployed. Men could learn new skills, such as shoe-repairing and carpentry, participate in musical and dramatic activities and keep fit.

An interesting insight into the ethos of settlements was provided by Horace Fleming, the founder and first warden of the settlement in Birkenhead:

The environment which a Settlement seeks to provide is that of fellowship. In its warmth, many a dwarfed and sullen spirit has budded and flowered into a valued personality. It is something more than the college atmosphere, though that is part of it. It is a thing of the spirit, and in its glow men are freed, for a time, from their bondage to sect, party or class, and become members of a family.[20]

Settlements were often badly equipped, the tutors not well paid and the buildings in a poor condition. All settlements struggled for funding, including the Letchworth Settlement. The term 'settlement' also became a problem, being associated with the Victorian patronage of Toynbee Hall and other social settlements, which some saw as patronising. The ESA was renamed the Educational Centres Association in 1946, acknowledging that the term 'settlement' was seen as unacceptable. Later, settlements faced competition from the community centres and community associations that were established on many of the new housing estates in the inter-war period, under the auspices of the National Council for Social Services (NCSS).[21] These organisations were seen as more egalitarian and democratic. Another point of conflict highlighted by Freeman is that the liberalism of the ESA's executive was often at odds with the Labour and socialist affiliations of many of the grass-roots leaders.[22]

The 1944 Education Act required local authorities to provide adult-education facilities and by 1948 all the surviving settlements received some financial help from their local education authority. These bodies also developed their own centres, providing yet another threat to the settlements. Writing in 2004, Freeman describes some of the surviving settlements:[23] the Bristol Folk House combines arts and crafts and language courses with exhibitions and musical events;[24] the Percival Guildhouse in Rugby puts on informal courses, including family history, and there is a licensed social club;[25] the Swarthmore centre in Leeds offers courses in computing, the arts and healthy living;[26] Letchworth Settlement has many similarities with these other institutions. Freeman writes: 'The surviving educational centres remain community resources, very different in scale and scope from the visions of the settlement pioneers.'[27]

The curriculum in the early settlements was heavily influenced by religion, but the use of their premises by WEA and university extension courses widened the scope, to include international relations, economics, literature, history, science and nature. Several had musical and dramatic societies.[28] There were common elements, including at Letchworth, such as a meeting room where students could enjoy fellowship as well as learning; the ESA's journal was originally called *The Common Room*. It was also felt important to foster a spirit of citizenship and to train voluntary workers for future social service.[29] Another frequent element was a Student Association, known in Letchworth as the Fellowship; there were often tensions between this group and the governing body of the organisation.[30]

The settlement movement was an important element in the provision of adult education, especially for those who had not had the opportunity to study. Although the numbers have declined, those settlements that have survived, like Letchworth, have done so because they have been able to adapt and to provide a range of classes and other activities that are popular and relevant.

Endnotes

1 <http://infed.org/mobi/adult-schools-and-the-making-of-adult-education/>.
2 Freeman, M, 'The decline of the adult school movement between the wars', *History of Education*, vol 39, no 4, 2010.
3 Quoted in Freeman, ibid., p. 488.
4 Freeman, M, 2010.
5 Freeman, M, '"An advanced type of democracy"? Governance and politics in adult education, c 1918–1930', *History of Education*, vol 42, no 1, 2013.
6 Barber, E, 'Settlements and Society', essay for the Certificate in Creative Writing II, 2016.
7 <https://en.wikipedia.org/wiki/Arnold_Toynbee>.
8 Barber, ibid.
9 Quoted in Barber, ibid.
10 <https://www.oxforddnb.com/view/10.1093/ref:odnb/9780198614128.001.0001/odnb-9780198614128-e-27646?rskey=vhvPdq&result=2>.
11 <https://www.toynbeehall.org.uk/about-us/our-history/>.
12 Barber, ibid.
13 <https://www.swarthmore.org.uk/about-us>.
14 <https://archiveshub.jisc.ac.uk/search/archives/0955d6d2-a74b-36f4-8d83-f82a9072f3ec>.
15 <https://www.woodbrooke.org.uk/about/about-woodbrooke-2/; https://www.fircroft.ac.uk/110-years>.
16 Freeman, M, <http://infed.org/mobi/educational-settlements/>; *The Joseph Rowntree Charitable Trust*, 2004.
17 Copy held at the Settlement, with other papers collected by Roy Evans.
18 Ibid.
19 Ibid.
20 Fleming, H, *Education through Settlements*, Beechcroft Bulletin No 4, Birkenhead, 1922, quoted in Kelly, T, *A History of Adult Education in Great Britain* (Liverpool), 1992, p. 264.
21 <https://www.ncvo.org.uk/centenary/>.
22 Freeman, M, 2013.
23 Freeman, M, 2004.
24 <https://www.bristolfolkhouse.co.uk/>.
25 <https://directory.warwickshire.gov.uk/service/percival-guildhouse>.
26 <https://www.swarthmore.org.uk/>.
27 Freeman, M, <http://infed.org/mobi/educational-settlements/>, 2002.
28 Freeman, M, 2002, p. 248.
29 Ibid. p. 255.
30 Ibid. pp. 257–8.

Chapter 2

THE EARLY YEARS, 1920–1925

T he new town of Letchworth (Garden City), originally just known as Garden City, was founded in 1903 and its history has been well documented.[1] As the world's first garden city, it has been studied extensively and many of its ideas have been copied around the world. It was more than a place where people could live in nice houses with gardens and good community facilities; income from commercial and residential rents was reinvested in the town, which attracted mainly working-class people seeking a better life. It became known in the early days for its eccentric characters, but a thirst for education was evident from the start.

The first reference to an adult school was in 1905 and classes were held in the Howard Hall from January 1906. Initially they were for men only, but at the AGM on 27 September 1906, women were admitted. The following year, when the population of the town was about 4,000, meetings were held at the Skittles Inn, Letchworth's famous 'pub with no beer'. This was designed by the two principal architects of the garden city, Barry Parker and Raymond Unwin, and opened on 8 March 1907. Its proprietors were Aneurin Williams and Edward Cadbury, both directors of First Garden City Ltd, and its manager was Bill Furmston.[2] Facilities included a skittles alley, billiard table and reading room. The adult school held meetings to discuss various esoteric subjects, such as the 'Utopias of More and Morris', 'The Mind's Apprehension of Divinity', 'The Political Position of Women' and the 'Fallacy of Neo-Malthusianism'.[3] It closed as an independent organisation in 1934, but continued to meet at the Settlement until about 1951.[4]

A recently published edition of letters between a conscientious objector in the first world war, Frank Sunderland, and his wife contains several references to the adult school. Lucy Sunderland was heavily involved and served on its committee. On 12 November 1916, for instance, she tells her husband about going to hear Sylvia Pankhurst speak.[5] The book is peppered with references to various talks she had heard at the 'Skittles' and to the adult school. The adult school also offered practical help, for example organising classes to teach people to mend their own boots.[6] It was also reported that a local woman gave money so that unemployed workers, who had come to the town looking for work, could be given a meal and a hot drink.[7]

In 1913 a new railway bridge was built over Norton Way North and the 'cattle creep', a path which had given access to the Skittles Inn from the railway station, closed. This badly affected the pub's trade and in 1923 it moved to the 'People's House' in Station Road, now the Job Centre. The building on Nevells Road remained empty until 1925 when the Adult Educational Settlement bought it. But that is to jump ahead.

The Letchworth Settlement, which is celebrating its centenary in 2020, was founded by members of the Quaker meeting house, 'Howgills', as an adult education school. Although there were similarities to other settlements, referred to in chapter 1, the Quaker links were not so important. Its original home was the former Letchworth Museum in Broadway, renting rooms from the Naturalists' Society.[8]

The first step in establishing the Settlement was to invite subscribers to finance the venture. Some of these people would have attended lectures but others were motivated by altruism and the view that improved education was something to be encouraged. Until permanent premises were found, expenses included rent and lecturers' fees. There must have been considerable discussion before the Settlement began life, but the records do not reflect this.

The first minute book of the governing body begins with a list of those involved.[9] The first warden was James Dudley, MSc, the chairman Dr R H Crowley[10] of Sollershott West and the secretary Alec B Hunter, the son of Edmund, owner of the St Edmundsbury Weaving Works. There were representatives from the Letchworth Elementary School Council, the Educational Settlements Association (ESA) and the Letchworth Evening Schools.

The first recorded meeting was that of the Finance Committee, held on 16 April 1920; the minutes are very brief but give a list of people to be approached for a £5 subscription. A committee meeting was held a week later, at St Brighids, Edmund Hunter's house in Sollershott West.[11] The first public meeting, referred to in chapter 1, was held on 8 May 1920 in the Howard Hall, when the speakers were Albert Mansbridge, secretary of the World Association for Adult Education, and C Ernest Alcock, secretary of the ESA. About 200 people attended, a considerable number for a small town.[12]

At a business meeting on 9 July, held at Barry Parker's studio, Dr Crowley, Barry Parker and Alec Hunter were appointed as trustees and entered into a lease with the museum, which they were to occupy from 12 July; the accommodation comprised all the rooms on the first floor, plus the entrance hall on the ground floor; the museum occupied the rest of the ground-floor rooms. The lease was for three years at an annual rent of £75. The warden outlined his plans: a six-month course was to cost 5s, to include use of the reading room; a three-month course would cost 2s 6d. He was authorised to submit a weekly article to *The Citizen* and the *Herts Express* newspapers. At the next meeting, held at the same venue three weeks later, the warden was asked to represent the Settlement as a vice president of the Letchworth branch of the League of Nations Union.[13]

The Settlement first opened to register intending students on 19 July 1920. People were invited to become subscribers, as the only way to raise money for the Settlement, and this entitled them to join the classes. Even today, no one can attend a class without becoming a member. The first annual report, described in more detail below, refers to the need to raise funds and that the Settlement depended almost entirely on private subscriptions.[14] The final page of the report lists the subscribers and provides a cash statement for the period 1 May 1920 to 30 April 1921. The subscribers included many well-known names, not just in Letchworth, such as two members of the Cadbury family, Miss Lawrence (the owner of 'The Cloisters' in Barrington Road), Mr A Mansbridge[15] and Mr B Seebohm Rowntree. Other local 'worthies' were involved, such as R W Tabor, sometime vice chairman of the Urban District Council and after whom Tabor Court is named, who was appointed as treasurer in January 1922.

From the very first, the teaching of handicrafts was seen as important and an early meeting of artist-craftsmen and others was held to consider suggestions for encouraging this.[16] There were several public lectures in September 1920, which drew high attendances, as many as 130. The following month saw the first class in music appreciation, held at 16 Common View and led by Mary Ibberson.[17] She later became sub-warden but left the Settlement to found the Rural Music School movement.[18]

Also in October, the warden presented a draft constitution and reported very favourably on the opening of classes in Letchworth and one at Arlesey, with the possibility of another at Baldock.[19] It was felt that another £200 needed to be raised, in order to free the warden to work full time for the Settlement. By the end of the year, the property was insured for £100, the constitution was agreed and it was decided to affiliate to the Educational Settlements Association. The following February it was agreed to join the World Association for Adult Education, but a decision on joining the National Council for Social Service was postponed.

The Citizen reported on the first social gathering and conference, in its edition of 17 December 1920.[20] This was held at the museum on 11 December and the speakers were the warden, who spoke about the work of the Settlement in Letchworth and in the neighbouring district, and Professor Cock, of University College Southampton, whose subject was

LIST OF SUBSCRIBERS.

Aitcken, Miss
Amor, Miss R.
Bartholomew, Mrs.
Bell, Mr.
Blair, Misses
Bond, Mrs.
Branson, Mrs.
Brown, Mr. F. H.
Browne, Mr. G. W. W.
Cadbury, Mr. E.
Cadbury, Mr. G.
Cartwright, Miss
Clapham, Mr. H. D.
Clapham, Mrs., Senr.
Clapham, Miss
Clapham, Miss K. L.
Colebrook, Mrs.
Colebrook, Miss M. B.
Corsellis, Miss
Crees, Miss
Crowley, Dr. R. H.
Crowley, Mrs.
Cubbon, Rev. and Mrs.
Dent, Mr. J. M.
Derry, Mrs.
Dewe, Miss
Dodge, Mr. and Mrs.
Evans, Mr. Alfred
Firth, Miss
Grace, Mrs.
Gregory, Mr. E. E.
Hoffman, Mr. and Mrs.
Holden, Miss
Howlett, Miss K.
Hunter, Mr.
Ibberson, Mrs.
James, Mr.
Jewson, Miss
King, Miss
Lander, Mr. and Mrs.
Latchmore, Mr. G. H.

Lawrence, Miss
Leakey, Mr. James
Macfadyen, Dr. and Mrs.
Macfadyen, Mrs. D.
Mansbridge, Mr. A.
Matthews, Mrs. P.
Matthews, Mrs.
McGraw, Mrs.
Menzies, Miss
Middleton, Mrs.
Moss, Miss
Napier, Misses
Parker, Mr. and Mrs. B.
Payne, Mr. William
Pearsall, Mrs. E. B.
Pearson, Mrs.
Priestman, Mr.
Penrose, Mr.
Prentice, Mrs.
Pym, Miss R.
Ransom, Miss
Rea, Miss Hope
Rodgers, Mrs.
Rodgers, Mrs.
Rowntree, Mr. B. Seebohm
Shannon, Miss
Smith, Mrs. Vine
Spicer, Miss C.
Steen, Dr. W. C.
Sugden, Miss
Taylor, Miss
Theosophical Educational Trust
Tillyard, Miss
Tothill, Miss
Warner, Mr.
Warner, Miss A.
Weekes, Mr.
Weight, Mrs.
Williams, Mr. Aneurin
Wiltshire, Mr. H.
Young, Miss

6

1   List of subscribers, from first annual report, 1921. GCC 2018.21.1.1e

'The meaning of education'. According to the article, Letchworth was in the unique position of being the only settlement which included outlying villages in its lecture programme.

The first AGM was held on 22 January 1921 and covered in *The Citizen* a few days later.[21] The warden reported that in the first term there were nine courses of lectures at five different centres; two were held at Arlesey and Baldock, and students came from Hitchin, Radwell, Stotfold and St Ippolyts. One of the history courses was arranged by the WEA and another by the Pearsall Trust.[22]

The Settlement was fully covered in the local press and *The Citizen*, in its 15 July 1921 edition, gave a detailed report on the work during the first year:

The Letchworth Adult Educational Settlement was opened in the autumn of 1920 with the object of meeting the growing need for education among the men and women of the locality... The aims of the movement, and of the Letchworth Settlement in particular, may be said to be twofold: (1) to provide facilities for adult education of as high a quality and of as wide a character as possible. (2) to work for the development of the personality of the individual, through association in groups for study, discussion and the exchange of information and varying points of view...[23]

The first annual report is worth quoting at length, as it set out the purpose of the Settlement:

The Letchworth Adult Educational Settlement was opened in the autumn of 1920 with the object of meeting the growing need for education among the men and women of the locality... It is becoming increasingly evident that, as the nineteenth century saw the extension of educational facilities to the whole of the childhood of the nation, so, during the twentieth century, must these facilities be further extended so as to include the nation's manhood and womanhood. What was a luxury for the few has become a necessity for the many in these days of widened social, economic and political responsibility.[24]

It went on to say that there had been seven courses of twenty or more lectures, on a variety of subjects such as modern history, geology, chemistry, music appreciation and economics. There was also a short course on English literature and a class on industrial history, arranged by the WEA.[25]

At the end of the first month there were 150 students with an average attendance of about two-thirds of those enrolled on the courses. During the summer two new courses started: a Dramatic Reading Circle met weekly, with an average attendance of nearly thirty, and read plays by Ibsen, Shaw, Stanley Houghton and John Drinkwater, followed by a discussion. A course of lectures on Regional Survey, arranged in conjunction with the Letchworth Naturalists'

Society, had an average attendance of about 27 and resulted in the formation of a practical Regional Survey Group.[26]

The governing body had an equal number of subscribers and students. The Students' Fellowship was seen as a way of drawing together the students attending different classes and thereby creating a 'Settlement spirit', which was seen as important in all settlements.

There was a programme of single lectures, including 'Relativity', 'Art in education', 'Industrial art' and 'Education and democracy'. The lecture on relativity was given by Mr E Cunningham, Director of Studies at St John's College, Cambridge and, according to *The Citizen*, the lecture room was crowded.[27] More importantly, perhaps, it was a financial success.[28]

In March 1921 Barry Parker succeeded Dr Crowley as chairman. Despite the almost permanent financial difficulties, plans were made to buy a piano and to buy or hire a car in order to continue the village classes. In July it was agreed to hire a car at a cost of about £36, and students in the villages were to be asked to contribute. And there were the regular expenses, including rent and tutors' fees. By this time there were 500 subscribers, which was an impressive figure so early in the Settlement's life. Two months later it was decided to buy a second-hand piano for £40.

The 18 November 1921 edition of *The Citizen* spoke fulsomely about the Settlement:

> To those who are not in the inner circle of the Letchworth Adult Educational Settlement, that organisation is known principally as the power which draws eminent lecturers to Letchworth, so that even those who are not members of the Settlement may be kept in touch with the main current of intellectual life in this country. As so many people pass their lives in the mere backwaters only, the Settlement is rendering excellent service to Garden City in bringing people here from the principal centres of light and learning.[29]

Local partiality aside, it is clear that the classes and single lectures offered to citizens were of a very high standard. The following year *The Citizen* reported on the third winter session, about to start, and began the article with some notes on the Settlement's general aim and constitution:

> It is a body supported entirely by voluntary subscriptions and donations for the purpose of providing further opportunities for education for all men and women who feel their need of it, irrespective of party, creed or social class. The type of education aimed at is not "high brow" or bookish, but such as whilst extending the knowledge of the student, will also widen his interests and understanding and make for a well balanced life. With this end in view, free discussion and the fellowship and comradeship which come from the frequent meeting together of groups with a common desire are felt to be essential, whatever subject

is being studied. The students themselves take a large share in the government of the Settlement, appointing half the Council from their own number. The fees for the classes are very low in order that no-one may be prevented from taking advantage of them, and it cannot be too strongly emphasised that all, manual workers and middle class alike, are equally welcome to share in the education it offers…Very few places in the country, probably no town as small as Letchworth, can offer such advantages…[30]

As the warden was submitting articles for the local press, he may have suggested what might be included, but it seems clear that the Settlement was seen to be new and exciting by citizens and this is reflected in the coverage of its activities.

In the early days of the Settlement, it is clear that lots of things were happening. In February 1922, for example, approval was given for a summer pageant, for the purpose of 'propaganda'[31] and to raise funds; the Brotherhood Dramatic Society, the folk dancers and a madrigal society were invited to take part, but it was not in fact held that year. The warden reported that a conference of those engaged in settlement work was to be held in Letchworth on 20 May 1922; he also reported that Miss Lawrence had offered the use of her premises, the Cloisters, for classes. The warden proposed camping as a new activity, beginning with a small weekend camp in the summer.

By November, the warden was reporting that the Settlement was busier than ever, with more classes and students. There were new village classes at Stotfold and Radwell, and there had been requests from Meppershall, Henlow, Ashwell and Weston. At the AGM, held on 10 November, the chairman expressed great satisfaction with the growth of the Settlement 'on such firm lines of education, fellowship and co-operation'. He rather grandly pointed out that this was the way a new social order would be evolved.[32] The first world war had ended four years previously and had had a profound effect on the country. Some women had finally been enfranchised in 1918 and a lot of deference to those seen as superior was no longer regarded as appropriate.

At the Council meeting on 23 November 1922 it was reported that the Citizens Welfare Committee[33] was trying to find suitable premises and was considering building its own centre. It had identified a plot of land at the corner of Leys Avenue and Norton Way and Barry Parker was asked to prepare plans. However, its funds were insufficient and discussions were held with the Settlement about sharing the premises, with the Settlement becoming tenants. There was also a suggestion that the Settlement could share the new Skittles Inn on Station Road but this was felt to be undesirable. Barry Parker wanted to amalgamate the museum, library and Settlement in one block of buildings and there was also the first suggestion of buying the old Skittles Inn on Nevells Road. A special meeting of the executive committee was held on 18 December

1922, at which the warden was given permission to work with the Citizens Welfare Committee. A strong supporter of the Welfare Committee was Norman Macfadyen, chairman of Letchworth Urban District Council, and he was very keen to have a new facility for the Committee and Settlement in one building. It was eventually decided to ask the Naturalists' Society to allow the Settlement to remain at the museum for another three months.

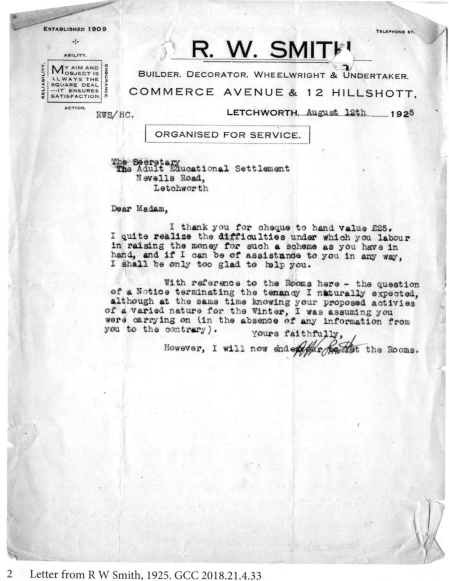

2   Letter from R W Smith, 1925. GCC 2018.21.4.33

By the following May the warden had reported on his search for other suitable premises, but none was available at a lower rent than was currently being paid. However, it was stated in March 1924 that the UDC proposed to take over the premises in the museum during the autumn or winter, in order to provide a public library, and notice to quit was to be given on 24 June. Efforts to find a new home redoubled: in May 1924 it was reported that the executive committee had looked at the 'Garden City Hotel'[34] and considered it very suitable. A sum of £3,000 had been refused and the committee was willing to go up to £3,750, but the owners of the hotel wanted £6,500. Enquiries were made about accommodation in the flats over Mr Rodgers' shop in Leys Avenue at a rent of £100 a year. Clearly the idea of purchasing the former Skittles Inn was being discussed, but in June it was reported that it was unclear when the premises would be available and there was a need for temporary accommodation until then. It was agreed to take half of Mr Rodgers' upstairs premises at an inclusive rent of £60 for up to three months. This too fell through, as Mr Rodgers wanted £100 for the whole flat. The only other premises available were those lately occupied by the Book Club over Mr R W Smith's premises in Commerce Lane, at a weekly rent of 28s.[35]

At a special executive committee meeting on 17 July 1924, it was reported that the Skittles Inn was for sale and that an offer must be made immediately, at an amount not to exceed £2,300. Two months later the committee was told that the premises could be bought for £2,000 but Mr Cadbury insisted that no sale should take place until the premises were in full working order. The question of the sale dragged on, but in November it appeared to be fairly certain that the Settlement would have first refusal. In December the warden said that the sum of £2,000 would be accepted and urged that the premises be purchased. A fresh lighting and central heating system would be necessary, but it was felt that the students could undertake any redecoration required; he also thought two-thirds of the purchase price could be raised by a mortgage and this was agreed. A special executive committee meeting was held on 5 January 1925, to consider arrangements for the purchase. Three trustees were appointed, Dr Crowley, Barry Parker and Mr Tabor; two more were to be added and empowered to complete the purchase. It was agreed that the opening ceremony should be a prestigious event and there were discussions about who might perform it. A month later it was hoped to take possession after 7 March and there was discussion of a new name; suggestions included naming it after Dr Crowley or Dr Mansbridge. At a joint council and executive committee meeting on 14 March 1925, it was reported that a building society had agreed to a mortgage of up to £2,000, repayable over twenty years at an interest rate of 6 per cent.[36] It was felt that a lower rate could be obtained

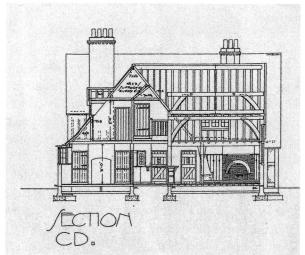

3   Plan of Skittles Inn, August 1906. The plan shows the two floor layouts, with sections and elevations. GCC plan 1707

4   Brunt Room with billiard table, nd.

elsewhere, 'but as there were other reasons for using this society & the Settlement was committed to Dr Mansbridge the loan was agreed to'. There was further discussion about a name, Dr Crowley declining the honour, and suggestions included 'Icknield House' and 'Nevell's House'; in the event 'The Settlement' was agreed on, which it had been called in its previous premises, with a sub-title of 'Community Centre For Adult Education'. A Mr and Mrs Sales were willing to act as host and hostess and live in the building; they offered £50 a year (presumably for rent) and would live on the second floor.[37] The museum asked if it could have the old sign, which was agreed so long as it was replaced.

During the search for new premises and the occupation of the old Skittles Inn, the work of the Settlement continued. In October 1923 the warden reported that he had been invited by the County Council to give a series of lectures on Saturday mornings to schoolteachers; he also reported that the Thomas Wall Education Trust had given a grant of £100.[38] The following January the warden said that about thirty teachers were attending the new lectures. In March the Settlement was invited to send a representative to the committee for promoting a Civic College; this particular idea rumbled on for several years, but never came to fruition. The plans were extensive; it was to be built on Town Square

THE SKITTLES INN
FOR EDUCATION

DEAR SIR, OR MADAM—Your interest in the development of Letchworth Garden City will, we are sure, be extended to one of its institutions, THE ADULT EDUCATIONAL SETTLEMENT. Its purpose and progress are well described in the last Annual Report which was printed in a recent issue of "The Citizen," and an extract from which is appended.

Briefly, the Settlement is a Community Centre at which men and women can find that kind of educational help which makes for good citizenship in the fullest sense of the word.

Since the Report was issued, the progress has been rapid, and the need for more adequate premises has become acute. It therefore gives us pleasure to announce that this need is now being met by the securing of The Skittles Inn for the Settlement.

5 & 6   Details of accommodation at Skittles Inn, Feb 1925. GCC 2018.21.1.50

This valuable property has been obtained at a price even below the pre-war cost of building. The facilities offered in the premises are ideal for the particular work of the Settlement, and will provide for :

A GOOD COMMON ROOM,

A LIBRARY FOR QUIET STUDY,

SEVERAL LARGE AND ATTRACTIVE LECTURE ROOMS,

ROOMS ADAPTABLE FOR HANDICRAFT WORK,

ACCOMMODATION FOR CARETAKER,

LARGE GARDEN SUITABLE FOR OUT-OF-DOORS FUNCTIONS

Not only, therefore, will the present classes be more suitably accommodated, but there will also be increased opportunity for forming other classes which are desired, but for which it has, up to the present, been impossible to provide.

We are asking for a sum of £3,000 to provide for the purchase, necessary alterations and equipment ; and in view of the support given to the Settlement during the four and a half years of its existence, and the increasing interest in Adult Education, both in Letchworth and in the country at large, it is confidently expected that this appeal will meet with a generous response.

To those who feel that they could also assist in raising additional sums, we would suggest the following methods for consideration :

1. Proceeds of Concerts, Sales of Work, etc.
2. Collection from friends who are interested.
3. Collection at meetings of other institutions.

Contributions for this object will be gratefully received by the officers of the Council :

R. BARRY PARKER, *Chairman*

RUTH I. PYM, *Secretary*

EMILY M. WALLER, *Secretary of Purchase Fund*

ALICE E. BROOKE, *Financial Secretary*

CHARLES S. ROWDEN, *Chairman of Students' Fellowship*

JAMES DUDLEY, *Warden*

Or the Treasurer, R. W. TABOR, Station Place, Letchworth.

February, 1925.

and to have lecture rooms, laboratories, a swimming pool and gymnasium, open to all residents.[39] The 'Colours Committee' recommended that deep yellow and brown be adopted as the Settlement colours.

The Hertfordshire Express, on 6 December 1924,[40] gave a full account of the AGM, held at the Church Room, Commerce Avenue.[41] It gave details of the warden's annual report, in which he had looked for answers to the questions: 'To what extent are the hopes of the founders being realised?', 'Has the experiment been justified?' and 'Has there been awakened a desire for the kind of educational help which the Settlement was instituted to provide, and is that desire extending and deepening?' He said that each year had seen an increase in the number of classes and subjects studied, as well as the number of tutors. During the previous year nine tutors had conducted weekly classes, compared with two in the first year, and the curriculum had grown. He continued:

> It is significant to note that, whereas in the early days of the Settlement it was necessary to create or awaken an interest in education before a class could be started, today requests for help are coming to us, and a class already in existence assumes as a matter of course that it will continue… Our problem is now to meet satisfactorily the desires we have aroused. In terms of supply and demand, we have proved beyond question that the demand is genuine and increasing; we shall have difficulty in maintaining an increasing supply.

A magazine called *The Worker*, in its issue of 18 December 1924,[42] said that the Settlement did not usually concern itself with its students' occupations, 'holding that its function is to offer opportunities for developing a fuller wider life to all who desire it, irrespective of their walk in life'. However, it added:

> Some interesting facts have been brought to light through an inquiry into students' occupations, undertaken at the instigation of the Board of Education. It showed that bricklayers, gardeners, parsons, agricultural labourers, clerks, cooks, shop assistants, railway porters, station masters, householders, farmers, glove machinists, electrical engineers, school teachers, factory hands and many others are meeting together on the common ground of the Settlement Classes, united by a common desire for real intercourse, wider knowledge and a deeper understanding of life, and, in many cases, for beauty and the opportunity for self-expression.

Letchworth was essentially an industrial town and this shows how many manual occupations were represented. It also confirms the desire for education referred to already. However, it was not all serious study; *The Citizen* said, in February 1924, 'Much has been said and written on the subject of the Adult Educational Settlement at work; but last Saturday saw a somewhat lighter side of its activities. About fifty students assembled at the Museum Buildings, and the meeting opened with the singing of "The Wraggle-Taggle-Gypsies O"... judging from the reception given to the first speaker it is strongly to be recommended as a means of arousing enthusiasm...'[43]

The new premises were officially opened in September 1925 by the Hon. Oliver Stanley, private secretary to the Minister of Education, and Major Kindersley, MP for North Hertfordshire. It was described as a 'House Warming'. In his address at the opening, the warden reviewed the work since 1920:

In September 1920, the Settlement only existed in the minds of a small group of people, and the first class consisted of twenty-one students. Gradually extending the work, the number reached four or five hundred regular students, and there was every prospect of a thousand being enrolled before long. The Settlement was started in faith and had justified itself. The Settlement work was not confined to Letchworth, it had inaugurated classes in other places where transport was difficult and the many distractions of Letchworth life were absent... It would be seen from these aims that the Settlement was seeking to provide something that was notably lacking in our social order, which no "ism" could supply. Through hard thinking and devoted service alone could we gain knowledge, reach higher ideals and form character.[44]

The event was covered in *The Citizen* on 25 September 1925; it reported Miss Ibberson saying that £1,500 of the purchase price had been repaid, so although the place was their own it still had to be paid for.[45]

By November 1925 the Settlement was established in its new home and the AGM, held on 21 November, used the new centre for the first time. It was reported that many people had given furniture, pictures and china and the Meppershall class had given a chair for the common room. At the last meeting of the year, representatives from a number of bodies were invited to join the Council, including the Women's Co-operative Guild, the WEA, Hertfordshire County Council and the Trades and Labour Council.

The Letchworth Adult Education Settlement began with ambitious plans and was supported by many of the leading figures in the town at the time. During its first five years, it clearly met a need and expanded beyond its initial capacity; finance was an ongoing problem, not really solved until 1995.[46] The year 1925 marked a watershed in its history; by acquiring its own premises, those running the organisation believed they could grow and develop as more people came to the town. Its continued existence a century later (ninety-five of those years at the Nevells Road site) would suggest that their hopes were met.

Endnotes

1   See, for example, Miller, M, Letchworth. *The First Garden City*, 2nd edn (Chichester), 2002.

2   <https://www.letchworthsettlement.org.uk/about-us/history/>.

3   Ibid.

4   Notes by Ken Johnson, held in Letchworth Library; the women's adult school did not close until 1986 (see chapter 5). The date at which the men's adult school closed is unclear.

5   Macdonald, K (ed), *The Conscientious Objector's Wife. Letters between Frank & Lucy Sunderland, 1916–1919* (Bath), 2018.

6   *The Citizen*, 'Every Man His Own Cobbler', 24 November 1916, p. 9, column 1 [information from Philippa Parker].

7   <https://www.letchworthsettlement.org.uk/about-us/history/>.

8   The two principal series of documents for the Settlement are the minutes from 1920 to 2014, and what are described as 'Record books', from 1920 to 1946. The latter were apparently compiled by Barry Parker's son Robert and contain newspaper cuttings, syllabuses, reports and related material. They can be found in the Garden City Collection at LS7 and LS1 & 2 respectively.

9   See chapter 7 for fuller information about some of the key figures.

10 He was the Senior Medical Officer of the Board of Education and is also referred to in chapter 1.

11 Now listed as grade II; see <https://historicengland.org.uk/listing/the-list/list-entry/1102818>.

12 Garden City Collection, 2018.21.1.53; notes from Roy Evans.

13 An organisation formed in October 1918 to promote international justice, collective security and permanent peace between nations, based on the ideals of the League of Nations.

14 Ibid., p. 5.

15 Albert Mansbridge was one of the pioneers of adult education in Britain and best known for his part in co-founding the WEA, serving as its first secretary until 1915; see <https://en.wikipedia.org/wiki/Albert_Mansbridge>.

16 Garden City Collection, 2018.21.1.53.

17 See her book, *For joy that we are here. Rural Music Schools 1929–1950*, published in 1977.

18 See chapter 7 for more on Mary Ibberson.

19 See chapter 4 for more information on work in the villages.

20 Garden City Collection, 2018.21.1.4.

21 Garden City Collection, LS 1A, record book.

22 Set up to foster the study of constitutional history.

23 Garden City Collection, 2018.21.1.17.

24 First annual report, 1920–21, GCC, 2018.21.1.1.

25 Ibid., p. 3.

26 Ibid., p. 4; see also <https://www.dfte.co.uk/ios/origins.htm for information on Regional Survey>.

27 *The Citizen*, 18 February 1921.

28 Garden City Collection, LS 7.

29 Ibid., 2018.21.1.22(9).

30 Ibid., 2018.21.3.1.

31 Presumably to spread the word and attract more subscribers.

32 Ibid., LS 7A.

33 It is not clear what this organisation was and none of the histories of the town appear to mention it.

34 It is difficult to know which building this referred to; it may have been the Simple Life Hotel in Leys Avenue, but there is no evidence to support this one way or the other.

35 R W Smith was a builder, decorator, wheelwright and undertaker.

36 Garden City Collection, LS 7D.

37 The building has two floors, so this must refer to the first floor.

38 For information on the Thomas Wall Education Trust see <https://www.thomaswalltrust.org.uk/>.

39 Details can be found in a typed document, dated February 1927; Garden City Collection, 2018.21.9.5C.

40 Garden City Collection, 2018.21.1.75.

41 It is not clear what building this refers to.

42 Garden City Collection, 2018.21.1.78; this was a newspaper produced in Letchworth between 1921 and 1930 with copies in the British Library newspaper collection.

43 Garden City Collection, 2018.21.2.72.

44 Ibid., LBM4074.15.13.

45 Ibid., 2018.21.5.4.

46 This was when the then Letchworth Corporation accepted the building as a gift and leased it back to the Settlement. This will be covered in more depth in chapter 5.

Chapter 3

GROWTH AND DIVERSIFICATION, 1926–1970

The inter-war years

In 1928 the Settlement published a small leaflet, describing eight years of adult education in Letchworth and the surrounding district.[1] In a foreword, Dr Ralph Crowley said that he was one of a group of people who took the initiative in 1920 to found the Letchworth Adult Education Settlement. The feeling uppermost in his mind was one of encouragement, believing that 'under the leadership of James Dudley, the Settlement has succeeded in realising in considerable measure the aims with which it set out'. He continued:

> What were the ideals and hopes of the early days? What was the special contribution that we hoped our Adult Educational Settlement would bring to the life of men and women, and to the community in Letchworth and the villages around? We had two main hopes, which together represent the essential in progress in man's development. Our first was that we might help one another in the realisation of our individual selves and in the enrichment of each one's personality. Our second, that we might realise these ends together, in the setting of the community, by the way of fellowship.

He concluded by saying that there was room in every direction for development: the need to consolidate the present work, to reach out to more people in Letchworth and to embrace a large number of nearby villages, 'and to weld into a unified whole all students and members of the Settlement'. He also saw a need to link up the Settlement's work with the education of the adolescent, and to give expression to the ideal of education working as a continuous process through the life of the individual. He believed that 'In this direction lies the path and the goal of true citizenship'. Dudley came in for special praise under the heading of 'Leadership': 'It would be difficult to over-estimate the importance of the right leadership in pioneer work of this kind. The Letchworth Settlement has been more than fortunate in having for its first

Warden Mr James Dudley, whose versatility and width of outlook have counted for so much in the first eight years of the Settlement's life'.[2]

The leaflet described the difficulties of the early years, especially finding suitable premises, and concludes: 'It says much for the spirit already in existence that the community was able not only to maintain its life but also to show an increase in the number of class enrolments during the year.' The attendance figures since the beginning are worth reproducing:

	Year	Classes	Enrolments	Subscribers
	(1st	8	121	81
Museum	(2nd	15	262	131
	(3rd	18	310	150
	(4th	18	325	154
Commerce Lane	5th	22	426	165
Present premises	6th	27	557	247
	7th	29	610	260

The debts incurred on purchasing the premises were described as a very serious burden: £600 of the mortgage still had to be found. The leaflet concluded with a quote from a report on adult education issued by the Ministry of Reconstruction, set up after the end of the first world war:

Adult Education must not be regarded as a luxury for a few exceptional persons here and there, nor as a thing which concerns only a short span of early manhood, but is a permanent national necessity, an inseparable aspect of citizenship, and therefore should be both universal and lifelong. The opportunity for Adult Education should be spread uniformly and systematically over the whole community, as a primary obligation on that community, in its own interest and as a chief part of its duty to its individual members, and therefore every encouragement and assistance should be given to voluntary organisations, so that their work, now necessarily sporadic and disconnected, may be developed and find its proper place in the national education system.[3]

Another view of the Settlement came from Mrs Wheeler, chair of the Students' Fellowship, who wrote an article for the in-house magazine in 1930, entitled 'What is the Settlement?':

The premises in Nevells Road are not all that could be desired, but the fact that they are equally unsuitable for nearly every purpose makes them equally adaptable for every kind of function imaginable. It is now more than five years since we took up our quarters at the Skittles Inn. Before that we were grateful for a couple of rooms over an undertaker's shop, and before them for a floor above the Museum...[4]

7   Duchess of Atholl dinner, 1926. None of the guests is identified, but Barry Parker is standing up at the back. GCC 701.107

The first full year in its new home saw a visit by the Duchess of Atholl on 28 January 1926; she was the Parliamentary Assistant Secretary to the Board of Education. A reception was held at the Settlement, followed by dinner at the Co-operative Hall, for which morning dress was required.[5] The *Herts Express* reported on the event on 6 February 1926, which was attended by 400 people, and on the Duchess's speech:

> Here [she said] they had a settlement which was alive to all its opportunities, with a large number of students in the town and country. She thought it was most appropriate that it should have taken root in Letchworth; she had felt that those who went out into the wilderness to found Garden Cities were people of independent thought – such people as would naturally strike out new lines in education. She was struck with the breadth of the studies provided at the Settlement.[6]

The financial situation continued to be of concern; it was reported at the 1926 AGM:

> This touches a side of Settlement life which has loomed very large during the last year, namely, the constant pressure of financial difficulty. This has been like the stone of

Sisyphus, the Settlement has managed to roll it some little way up the hill of solvency – at any rate, it has not crushed us. To wear down the debt on the building and to keep the general fund in that happy financial state so feelingly described by Mr Micawber, has, however, been an anxious task, especially for the treasurer and council.[7]

In January 1934 it was agreed to print 500 copies of an appeal leaflet, which the local printers J M Dent printed free of charge, and to send two copies to all the factories in the town, as well as to some shops. Another appeal in 1936 asked firms to tell their employees about the Settlement, as it would be particularly helpful for the young people who lived in lodgings and were often quite lonely.[8]

In 1926, the annual report said: 'A new element has been added to the Settlement by the opening of a canteen run by the Fellowship and especially organised by Mrs Wheeler. This has added very greatly to the comfort of the common room and has, moreover, been a source of income to the Settlement.'[9]

In May 1929 new caretakers were appointed, Mr and Mrs Mallett, staying in the post for three years. Their daughter, Edna, gave a long account of her time there to *Letchworth Recollections*:

My mother longed to live in Letchworth... The chance came in 1928, when a group of people from the Settlement came to Arlesey for an evening of talk and entertainment... The warden was looking for a resident couple to be caretakers, with the man working full-time in the factory. It was a tough life: Father had to stoke the central heating, look after the large garden, fruit trees and outside area, and help my mother with the cleaning. The flat upstairs was pleasant, but there was no kitchen, so we ate our dinner downstairs in 'The Classroom', next to the kitchen, and carried stuff upstairs for the evening meal. The bulk of the early members seemed to be educated people; school teachers featured largely; it was more a club for the intelligentsia,[10] and a fascinating crowd they were to us. My parents, though naïve in some ways, were intelligent, with a sound village common-sense. They sympathised with the Settlement ideals, but laughed at the lack of realism; much of it was a foreign language to ordinary people... A little money was made by renting out the premises to various groups. I was intrigued by the spiritualists, and lurked around hoping to see something unusual. They were mostly quite ordinary, but mother did cope now and again with the odd hysterical case...

One morning Bernard Shaw himself walked in, looking for someone, and my mother recognised him at once by his whiskers. Though we sometimes laughed at their ways, we were aware that these various people, Fabians, vegetarians, agnostics, atheists, Quakers, Anglo-Catholics, Esperanto enthusiasts, pacifists, morris dancers and lino-printers, really did look on all men as equal. My parents were never condescended to as caretakers, but regarded as friends and fellow-workers... Certainly some people in Letchworth had more money than others, but at the Settlement you would not have known it from their clothing or ornaments; they walked or rode bicycles, and used the same forms of address to everyone.[11]

In April 1926 the Educational Settlements Association asked if James Dudley could be released for three or six months to take over the work of visiting other centres and acting in an advisory capacity. The ESA felt strongly that he should be the first warden to start the scheme even though it would cause difficulties for Letchworth; they promised to provide a substitute to take over his lectures. The committee reluctantly agreed and in July Dudley stated that Martin Browne, late warden of Doncaster, would fulfil his teaching commitments for six months, with Miss Ibberson as acting warden.[12] However, two months later it was reported that Browne had withdrawn; at Dudley's suggestion it was decided to use visiting lecturers instead.

Dudley was clearly seen as a rising star; in March 1927 the World Association of Adult Education offered him two months in Germany and asked him to choose his own time in the spring term of the following year. In the event he did not return to Letchworth (see chapter 7). In September Mr H E Milliken of Malvern College was proposed as Dudley's successor, at a salary of no less than £400 a year, of which the ESA was to be asked to contribute £75 a year.

8   Woodcut of window and owl, from second newssheet, 1927. GCC 2018.21.8.32a

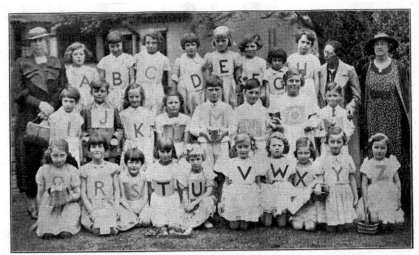

YOUNG FRIENDS OF THE MEMBER S OF LETCHWORTH SETTLEMENT WHO GAVE AN ALPHABET TAB-
LEAU AT THE SETTLEMENT'S ANNUAL FAIR ON SATURDAY. THE H ON, MRS. SEROCOLD, WHO OPENED
THE FAIR, IS ON THE LEFT, AND ON THE RIGHT IS MISS RUTH PYM, THE WARDEN.

9   Alphabet tableau at the summer fair, 1936. GCC 2018.21.17.153

There were many social events, often to raise money, and while some of the sideshows would be familiar today, others have fallen out of favour. Examples included 'Bunty pulls the strings', 'Chinese washing day' and 'haunted grotto'.[13] There was a summer fair most years, a pageant, as well as concerts and plays put on by the Settlement Players.[14]

Edna Mallett also talked about some of these events:

The Settlement certainly knew how to put on a show, in the form of the Summer Pageant… One year we had a gypsy pageant, where elderly ladies rehearsed what were meant to be wild Hungarian dances, ending with a twist and flinging of the arms… Then there were *'tableaux vivants'*, where characters were posed in a setting to look like paintings by Gauguin or Degas, or a Greek marble frieze. Maidens tugged a flower-bedecked bull to a temple while Evan Fletcher, looking Byronic, recited Keats' 'Ode on a Grecian Urn'!

A report of the 1931 fair appeared in the *Beds & Herts Pictorial*, in which Mr D B Cockerell, chairman of the Settlement Council, said:

Recently some people had been criticising the Settlement and saying that those who attended were those who could well afford to pay large fees. The Warden had analysed the people who were attending the classes and were connected with the Settlement, and had found that the greater number, or a very large percentage of them, belonged to the wage-earning class and it was not correct to say that the majority of the students were middle-class people who had ample income. Most of the people who attended the classes were people with very small resources and what the Settlement could give them was to them of very great importance indeed…[15]

Local people continued to support the Settlement; in June 1928 it was stated that:

Col and Mrs Pryor, of Weston, have kindly consented to loan from their own collection a number of pictures by well known artists which illustrate the development of certain tendencies in art. The works of such well known painters as A E John, Wilson Steer, David Muirhead, John and Paul Nash, A W Rich, will be represented and amongst the pictures by artists less known to the public in general will be examples of the work of Gwen John, Gwen Raverat and Col and Mrs Pryor…[16]

There were also displays of students' work, especially arts and crafts, such as an exhibition of paintings by working men and women in 1931.[17] In October 1933 the warden reported that a picture exhibition organised by the Sketch Club had been a great success; about 250 people had attended and a profit of £3-11-4 had been made.

There were a number of special events, but there is often no record beyond a brief reference. A 'World Trade Supper' was held in April 1933, for which a menu survives.[18] In January 1934 there was a report of a 'Newcomers' Social', apparently the third one to be held:

WORLD TRADE SUPPER.

M E N U.

Ostend Rabbit & Wiltshire Bacon.
Petits Pois.

Seville Orange Marmalade Tarts.

Swedish Ryvita. Dutch Cheese.
Danish Butter.

Chinese Figs. Tunis Dates.
Ginger & Muscatelles.
Jamaica Bananas. Brazil Nuts.

Kenya Coffee &
Nestlés Swiss Milk.

Vienna Bread.

10   International food supper menu, 1933. It shows an eclectic selection of foods but hardly a balanced menu. GCC 2018.21.15.86

These gatherings are primarily designed to give newcomers the opportunity of meeting residents and other newcomers, but they are equally for all who would like to extend their circle of acquaintances. The former meetings held have justified the experiment in that many newcomers have found friends in Letchworth much more quickly than they would otherwise have done.[19]

One curious idea was that of 'Diminishing teas'; it was estimated that this would raise at least £159-13-0 but in October 1925 it was reported that it had not been very successful.

During Civic Week 1935, held to mark George V's silver jubilee, the Settlement was responsible for one episode in the Pageant of Letchworth to be held at Letchworth Hall Hotel.[20] The council felt that during Civic Week more attention should be drawn to the necessity for preserving the beauty of the town: 'For the purpose, two cars, bearing large placards, one showing a Letchworth scene in an orderly condition and the other the same scene disfigured by papers and litter, should pass slowly through the streets.' After discussion, it was decided to ask the Civic Week Committee if it could supply a car for the purpose and to ask the Council for more waste-paper baskets.

In January 1937 one of the social events was a beetle drive, which was 'very popular in the North of England and is rapidly becoming the vogue in the southern counties'.[21]

The Ascot Training Centre regularly sent students to the Settlement, and in November 1930 a reception was held for them by the chairman of Letchworth Council, Mr A W Brunt.[22] 'After tea there were games and dances, with songs by Miss Joyce Goodman and Miss Fitzpatrick, while a recitation was given by Mr Kenneth Spinks. Mrs Gurney was at the piano. The trainees sang in Welsh, revealing that they have excellent voices.'[23]

The Settlement received practical help, such as the Ascot students making some new bookshelves for the library. Some firms also offered to help; in 1937 Lloyds offered to sell them an exhibition lawnmower for £2 10s, presumably a reduction on the usual price.[24]

In 1935 the House Committee felt that, in spite of the shortage of money, something should be done to make the Settlement more cheerful; material was bought for new curtains and cushions. Two years later, there were calls for a hall, with a fitted stage and other facilities, and this was referred to the AGM. The following March the Building Committee put forward proposals for a hall to accommodate 300, with a stage and moveable partition, so that part of the space could be used as an art room. The room would be about 30 feet by 80 feet and the cost was estimated at £1,330, with running costs of £108 15s per year. It was, however, felt that the overdraft must be greatly reduced before any further commitments could be undertaken; the subject was referred back to

LETCHWORTH SETTLEMENT

—◇—◇—◇—

DIMINISHING TEAS

—◇—◇—◇—

The scheme is started by one lady (A), who invites six other ladies (B's) to a tea party on the understanding that each guest will give her one shilling for the Settlement Purchase Fund and will herself as soon as possible give a tea party to five others (C's) on the same terms, except that each C will invite only four D's to her tea party, and so on *diminuendo* until each F hostess invites one guest. Thus:

1 A invites 6 guests.

6 B's each invite 5 guests.

30 C's each invite 4 guests.

120 D's each invite 3 guests.

360 E's each invite 2 guests.

720 F's each invite 1 guest.

As will be seen from the foregoing figures, if each hostess starts to collect her guests' contributions by herself putting down a shilling (as she will naturally wish to do) the scheme will contribute at least £159 13s. to the Purchase Fund.

Proceeds of each tea party should be sent to
Miss Ibberson, *Sub-Warden*,
The Settlement, Nevells Road,
Letchworth.

11 Diminishing teas, 1925. GCC 2018.21.5.3

the committee with instructions to prepare a further plan and estimate, and consider ways and means. In the event, it would be another twenty years before a new hall was realised.

Looking beyond Letchworth

Visits abroad began very early in the life of the Settlement. The first one, at Easter 1926, was to Normandy, most of the participants being students from the French class, and was thoroughly enjoyed.[25] In September 1927 the warden reported that a visit to Italy had been very successful; there were fourteen in the party, they had stayed in Florence and made excursions to Pisa, Siena and Fiesole. A visit to Belgium was also discussed and there was a further visit to France (Brittany) in 1928, which was thought to be one of the most successful.

```
        EASTER  TRIP  TO  BRITTANY.    1928


        On Thursday, April 5. under the leadership of Mr. and
Mrs. Dudley, a party of 14 students and friends left
Letchworth for Dinard, travelling by Southampton and
St. Malo.  At Waterloo we were joined by a party of eleven
(under Miss Cautherly) from the Wilmslow Settlement.  We
now numbered 27.  After a good crossing we reached St. Malo
about seven, landing an hour later.  We were ferried over
to Dinard, very ready for breakfast at the Hotel du Panorama.
This hotel, newly adapted as a W.T.A. centre is on the bay
so most of us had lovely views from our windows.
        This day, Friday, April 6. was spent resting or
strolling and exploring the neighbourhood, some of the
party taking a bus ride to St. Briac.
        Saturday, April 7. Two motor coaches took the party
to Mont St. Michel, passing through Dinan and Dol.  A most
interesting excursion which we hope to repeat. It rained
on the way back.
        Sunday, April 8. was a lovely warm day occupied by
church going and strolls.
        Monday, @pril 9. We went over to St.Malo, walking
on the walls of the old town. After Supper the Wilmslow
party entertained Letchworth with games.
        Tuesday, April tp 10. Several of us went to St. Malo
again, took the tram to St. Servan, which we found old and
picturesque, and then home by ferry.  These ferry journeys
are very delightful.
        Wednesday, April 11.A very strenuous day, for we went
to Dinan by the 8.15 boat. This is a delightful river trip
up the winding Rance. Here some visited the ramparts and
churches and others the castle. We got back to a late lunch
and packed, and after an early dinner the majority of the
party left Dinard by the 8.0'clock vedette.
```

12   Holiday to Brittany in 1928, giving a daily record of the week's activities. GCC 2018.21.9.29

In 1931, Mr Catchpole[26] of Welwyn Settlement invited Letchworth students to join a trip to some of the cathedrals of northern France; two Letchworth residents went on the trip, E Dear and N Larsen.[27] In 1936 there was a trip to Norway, under the auspices of the Garden City Town Planning Association.

The Settlement was not immune from events in the wider world. In May 1926 the building was thrown open to unemployed men and women during the General Strike. At the 1930 AGM the warden spoke on the settlement ideal, which he clearly felt contributed to a better world:

> …a training place which leads to the good life; to secure an educated democracy it was necessary that visibility and sympathy should be made effectual by knowledge. Co-operation between the young and older generation was needful, age bringing experience and wisdom. The Settlement is a practice ground for training in Citizenship wherein self-government can be learned and should foster the community spirit to serve too as a retreat whence inspiration may be drawn.

In 1931 the Educational Settlements Association declined to increase its grant to Letchworth, 'In view of the fact that they had many applications from distressed areas where there is a crying need for Classes.' Mr Fleming of the ESA said '[he] did not think that the ESA was in a position to give more help to Letchworth, where people had many other advantages & even the village classes, comprising some 90 students, were in good environments'. In reply he was told: 'There was a good deal of unemployment in Letchworth and many calls on people's purses in a new town which has no endowments to draw on; few people are wealthy and there is a specially large number of detached factory workers lodging in Letchworth away from their homes.' Mr Fleming asked if the Settlement was vital to Letchworth and Miss Pym, the then warden, replied that, being a growing factory town, it filled a place not provided by other organisations.[28] In September 1932, at Miss Pym's suggestion, it was agreed that the unemployed should be invited to attend a craft class on Friday evenings and have the free use of the hall for craft work and other purposes; also fees should be waived for unemployed students.

The 1934/35 annual report stated:

> Letchworth is a factory centre, not only a factory town, and workers come in from a radius of 10–15 miles to work here. Our factories now number 50, varying from Dent's Printing Works to Shelvoke & Drewry lorries, our biggest factories being Spirella and Kryn and Lahy steel works. Our students are drawn mainly from the factory and town offices, shops and factories – these account for 43%. 18% come from professions – mainly teachers, we have three elementary and four other schools. 22% are home workers and retired, unemployed and foreign students account for another 12%. A certain number of

these come in from neighbouring villages and towns like Baldock, Royston and Hitchin. We are trying to build up Music in the Settlement which since the days of Mr Dudley and Miss Ibberson has been in decline. There is a new tutor from Cambridge, Mr John King, who has worked up a strong and united class and Chamber Music concerts are being well attended.[29]

The age of the students was noted: twenty- to forty-year-olds predominated in the evening classes and there were very few young people in the afternoon ones, as might be expected if they were working. The Settlement was increasing its contact with the men from the distressed areas who were at the Ascot Government Training Centre and welcomed them free of charge: 'Some of them have attended the History and Psychology classes throughout the winter and have been keenly interested in the life of the Settlement'. The 1937/38 annual report said:

> Over 100 new members of classes and circles have been enrolled, among them being men and women who are in lodging in the town and trainees from the Ascot Government Centre. The Settlement is of special use to them apart from the classes they attend, as the Common Room gives them a place in which to prepare home-work and write letters, as well as affording an opportunity for making friends…

English for foreigners was being taught, with between twelve and fifteen students; they were German, Austrian, Hungarian, Swiss, French, Dutch, plus one man from Lancashire who wished to improve his English.

Individual students occasionally featured, usually when they had achieved something special. In July 1927 the warden told the committee that Miss Queenie Bowyer had been awarded a scholarship of £40 for the Working Women's College at Surbiton. In 1933 another student, A Scrutton, was awarded a travelling bursary of £7 and was going to France; the warden hoped that it could be made up to £10 and Mr Cockerell contributed 10s. Two years later Scrutton, described as 'a very keen student, particularly of languages', was applying for a scholarship to Ruskin College Oxford.

In December 1934 there were 379 individual students: 163 were attending Settlement classes, 128 ones put on by the County Council and 88 in the villages. A report, in June 1937, showed that fifty per cent of members were under thirty-five; the breakdown of occupations was very similar to the earlier survey.

New caretakers were appointed in May 1932, Mr and Mrs Ames, and in October 1935 a sub-committee, formed to consider possible economies, described their accommodation. It included three upstairs rooms, a bathroom, part of a loft, the downstairs scullery and use of the kitchen and classroom during the day as well as part of the garden. It was decided to create a self-contained flat, to free the kitchen and scullery for the sole use of the Settlement. In order to achieve this, it was proposed to install an electric cooker and substitute a sink for the hand-basin in the bathroom, partitioning off the toilet and installing a ventilator. New caretakers, Mr and Mrs Higgs, were appointed the following May.[30]

The second world war

Somewhat surprisingly, there is very little information about how the Settlement coped during the war. The first reference is to a Council meeting on 14 September 1939, when it was reported that the warden (John Short) was liable for military service but it was hoped that his work at the Settlement might have a prior claim. The Council 'were of the opinion that his work at the Settlement was of more National importance than Army service'.[31]

The president, Barry Parker, believed it was essential for the work of the Settlement to go on, and the rest of the committee agreed with him; the chairman was asked to seek permission from the police to hold meetings and black-out curtains were to be put up in the lecture room. The following month, it was reported that there was no problem with the Settlement opening as normal, subject to blackout regulations. Most classes continued and there was a social afternoon for evacuee mothers. In addition, the building was used on several days a week for schoolchildren and there were some classes solely for evacuees. It was decided not to dig an ARP trench, but to use nearby public shelters.[32]

An undated typed report, probably from 1939 to 1940, has a manuscript addition:

> And finally the opportunity presents itself for the Settlement Council to express its appreciation of the untiring and successful efforts which the Warden (assisted greatly by Mrs Short) has made, to keep the Settlement going in these unprecedented times of upset, strain and anxiety. So much depends upon the Warden, and we are sure that we have here the right man for the job.[33]

This is somewhat ironic, given what happened at the end of the war (see chapter 7).

The Common Room, the journal of the Educational Settlements Association, had an interesting article in its autumn 1939 issue which gives information that is not found in the Settlement's own records:

> Letchworth is in a Reception Area and they have as guests over 3,000 Londoners, for the most part mothers and small children. The Settlement has arranged various activities for them… An important class has just commenced in Hygiene and Mothercraft. This is taken by a doctor… there is an atmosphere of friendship and of concentration at the Settlement these days which the war has only intensified, not marred. There were fifty people in the Hygiene and Mothercraft class.[34]

1920 - 1941

THE PRESIDENT, OFFICERS AND COUNCIL
OF THE LETCHWORTH
ADULT EDUCATIONAL SETTLEMENT

request the pleasure of the company of

Mr & Mrs J P Westell

on the occasion of the

21ST BIRTHDAY CELEBRATIONS

to be held on

SATURDAY & SUNDAY, NOVEMBER 29 & 30

AT THE SETTLEMENT, NEVELLS ROAD

R.S.V.P.

PROGRAMME OVERLEAF

13   Invitation to twenty-first birthday celebrations, 1941. GCC LBM4074.15.247a

Settlement "Coming Of Age"

Personalities at the 21st birthday celebration of Letchworth Adult Educational Settlement. Seated (left to right): Miss H. M. Richards, Mr. R. Barry Parker, Mr. Arnold Rowntree, Dr. R. H. Crowley, Miss R. I. Pym. Standing (left to right): Mr. James Dudley, Mrs. Dudley, Mrs. Crowley and Mr. H. E. Milliken.

14   Twenty-first birthday celebrations, 1941, with photo of 'personalities'. GCC
LBM4074.15.217

In August 1940 it was reported that the Bloomsbury Technical College had been evacuated to Letchworth; it taught practical tailoring up to West End standard and it was felt to be a good idea to co-operate with it. In April 1941 a request was received from the Women's Voluntary Services for Civil Defence, asking for accommodation for the Evacuated Children's Clubs on three evenings a week. It was felt that the fifty Indian students being trained at the Letchworth Government Training Centre should be provided with adequate and carefully planned social activities, and lectures on English life and customs. Edna Mallett, whom we have already encountered, said:

> Amid all the entertainment, we became aware of sombre things: men and women with foreign names and accents were brought along and made welcome, and these, I was told, were 'refugees'. Russell Scott, who promoted the Esperanto classes, took several into his home. When unwelcome war-workers and evacuated teachers were dumped upon householders, they found a meeting-place and relaxation in the common room. Bewildered Indians, kitted out in navy suits, and training at the Government Centre to be artificers, had a social evening laid on for them. My mother took me along, aged 16, and the Indians and I found it an eye-opener. They were astonished that a decent white girl should be allowed to dance with them; I was surprised to hear that a society existed where it was forbidden.

In June 1941 the Hitchin & District Co-operative Society was allowed to use a room as an office for the Letchworth Town Milk Emergency Committee.

Somewhat unfortunately, the Settlement's twenty-first birthday fell in 1941 but, despite the war, it was decided to have some kind of celebration in October. Miss Pym, who had returned to the Settlement,[35] suggested a weekend, with addresses by various speakers on 'What the Settlement stood for and stands for'; there might also be a procession of characters in dress, revived from every pageant held at the Settlement. By all accounts, the celebrations went well.

In December 1942 the question of enlarging the building arose again, but was out of the question because of war restrictions on permits for material. At the AGM the following November there was a discussion about moving to a town-centre building and it was felt that immediate steps should be taken to alter and extend the existing one; the warden stressed the need for larger premises and advocated the building of a youth centre adjacent to the premises. There was further discussion over the next two years and ambitious plans for a new building near the grammar school on Broadway. There was a competition for a new name: nothing suitable was put forward but a small prize was awarded to a boy who had sent in several entries.

The annual report for 1942/43 reflected the hopes of the Settlement for life after the war:

Ambitious schemes are being considered for making the Settlement more and more the cultural centre of Letchworth, to meet the growing needs of a world in search of realities. It may be that after the War, the Settlement will grow out of all recognition, and will cover a much wider field than it does at present. It is for us to see that in the possible raising of our standards consequent upon the enlargement of our premises, and the widening of our interests, we do not discourage those people whose tentative efforts at self-expression have so far only reached their first shy beginnings, and to ensure that touch of intimacy and personal contact, that humanity and power of living together, which is the basis of all true culture, and is so much more important than all the academics in the world.[36]

At the AGM in November 1946 the chairman said that the previous year 'was a most successful one from every point of view', which he attributed to 'the fine spirit which is so characteristic of the Settlement and which is now so lacking in the world'. He stressed the tolerance and high ideals of the community and described the Settlement as 'an island of tranquillity in a sea of unrest'. The warden, Miss Richards (who had succeeded John Short at the end of the war), said that the past year had been her happiest of all: 'The extreme warmth radiated by the Students was mainly responsible for the fact that a neighbouring town was now agitating for a similar organisation.'[37] She said it was time to extend the work, 'for there could be no true democracy until we had an enlightened & educated people. We must combat defeatism, jealousy & hatred, raise humanity to a dignified level & cultivate a spirit of tolerance & good fellowship. Our main aim should be to train people to see the ethical issue in life.'[38]

Post-war activities

The 'Record books', from which much of our information derives, end in 1946, but there is a second series of scrapbooks, containing mainly newspaper cuttings and programmes of events up to October 1962. The minutes are the main source for the later history, but lack the spontaneity of the other material.

In August 1947 fifteen Settlement members had a 'memorable' holiday in Switzerland, staying in the Swiss chalet owned by the Settlement Council chairman, Mr Falk,[39] and enjoying the services of his cook–housekeeper. They had to pay their fares and five francs a day for food; the journey took thirty hours including the sea passage. A souvenir booklet was produced by L M Sadowski and A P Gay.[40] The *Herts Pictorial*, in its 26 August 1947 edition, contained an article about the trip. The leader of the party was Mr S W Palmer and he described the holiday to the newspaper:

The journey, especially through France, was their only unpleasant experience during the fortnight, Mr Palmer told me. It was very hot and the trains were dirty and crowded... Early each morning the party set out on a route they had planned the previous evening, roaming over mountains, through pine woods and exploring the mysteries of darkened caves…[41]

He referred to some amusing incidents. One example concerned the language barrier between the group and the local people: 'A request by Mr Palmer for a spray when they were troubled by flies was interpreted to mean a gun after various demonstrations.'

Despite Miss Richards' warm words quoted above, there was a serious falling-out in April 1948, leading to the resignations of the secretary, Miss Jones, the vice chairman, Florence Thompson, and a committee member, Kathleen Thompson; it was linked to a new constitution, although the actual details are unclear. The warden also resigned, 'as she felt that that body [the Management Committee] had violated the principles of justice, fair play and democracy. Her conscience would not allow her to remain…' Two of those who resigned were described as 'Martyrs to the New Constitution' and it appears that there had been disagreement over policy between the warden and the chairman of the committee, Mr Falk, and the treasurer, Mr Jefferies. The warden agreed to continue under a new constitution, but this was not the end of the story as her resignation was accepted after a vote.

At the 1950 AGM, the president, Mrs Harvey, described adult education centres in Germany which she had visited, and which she felt were doing valuable work in training citizens who would not be at the mercy of hysteria or propaganda. She added: 'In both countries, such centres were valuable clearing houses for conflicting views, and helped people to become articulate about

15   Party outside Swiss chalet, 1948.

their own convictions, which was highly important at a time when generally held opinions were being challenged by explicitly formulated theories.' She returned to the same theme three years later, at the AGM, when she spoke about another visit to Germany, particularly on the problem of young refugees and the failure of the west to prevent their being captured by communism:

> We did not show enough conviction and decision about what we valued, and were failing to make our civilization dynamic enough to appeal either to disillusioned German youth or to backward areas outside Europe. It was the duty of centres of adult education to take advantage of our precious heritage of freedom of speech to discuss fundamental issues and so create a community better fitted to meet the challenge of our times.[42]

Letchworth has three twin towns, one of which is Kristiansand in southern Norway; in 1954 a party of Norwegian visitors were entertained at the Settlement, although this predates the formal twinning. Sadly, there are no longer any reciprocal visits with Kristiansand, although they still continue with Chagny in France and Wissen in Germany.

The year 1953 saw a ten per cent cut in adult education, and the secretary was instructed to write to Nigel Fisher, the MP for Hitchin, as well as the Chancellor of the Exchequer and the Minister of Education, to protest at the cuts. There was some good news the following year, when the Settlement received a bequest

On 27th July 1954 the Club entertained their Norwegian visitors ▶
at a party in the Settlement.   'Hertfordshire Pictorial.'

16   Party of Norwegian visitors, 1954. GCC LBM3056.49.12

17 & 18   Kincaid Hall being built.

PROGRAMME
SATURDAY, 28th APRIL, 1956

The Hall will be officially opened at 7 p.m. by Dr. Myron L Koenig

Mr. John Loxham will be in the chair

Followed by entertainment by Settlement members

CHORAL AND ORCHESTRAL SOCIETY

ORCHESTRA
Conductor: Leonard Burbridge   *Leader:* Albert Weaver

Suite of Four Pieces	*Handel, arr. Dunhill*
March, Minuet 1, Minuet 2, Gavotte	
Air from Suite in D Major	*Bach*
Serenade from Quartet Op. 3, No. 5	*Hayden*
A Sword Dance Suite	*Arnold Foster*

A selection of music by the RECORDER GROUP, led by Ann Hales

THE MIMES GROUP directed by Mr. and Mrs. D. Booth

THE SETTLEMENT PLAYERS
present a play in one act
THE RING GAME, by Leonard de Franquen

CAST

MIRA, an old fishwife	*Kathleen Fitzpatrick*
PAPAGUILO, a baker	*Hugh Bidwell*
DOLFO, a fisherman	*John Cruse*
TORELLA, a handsome woman	*Jacqueline Smedley*
VOLINIA, an elderly woman	*Ella Edwards*
QUILO, a pawnbroker	*Stephen Ward*
NEPPI, a youth	*William Pearce*
FIGRETTE, a young girl	*Christa Topham*
VILLAGERS	*R. Buckstone, D. Fyfe, J. Innes, L. Lendorff*
	J. Ozels, J. Platten, P. Richardson, K. Wilson

Scene, a fishing village   ::   The play produced by K. Spinks

19 & 20   Brochure of the opening of Kincaid Hall (GCC 2018.21.29.5.3) and Dr Myron L Koenig, the US Cultural Attaché. The other guests are not identified. GCC LBM4074.8.8

from William Wallace Kincaid, co-founder of the US Spirella Company. The sum of £12,000 was split between the Settlement and the Civic Trust and it was decided to spend the money on building a new hall.[43] The successful tender was that of Messrs Fosters of Hitchin, at a cost of £4,052-12-6. In January 1956 it was reported that Dr Myron L Koenig, the US cultural attaché, was willing to open the hall – now named the Kincaid Hall – on 28 April, and this event was covered in the local press.

In 1960 a member of the Management Committee suggested changing the name of the Settlement to 'Centre of Art, Drama, Music and All Cultural Activities (CADMAC)' and the Settlement groups were asked to consider it; hardly surprisingly, most were against the idea. In 1962 there were discussions with the Urban District Council about joint plans for a civic theatre and arts centre. The long-serving warden, Roy Evans (who of course is still involved with the Settlement) was appointed in June 1963, and Mr and Mrs Higgs, the caretakers, left after twenty-seven years in the post. A portrait of Mr Kincaid was to be hung in either the hall or the green room. A selection of second-hand books from David's Bookshop was to be on sale for an experimental period on a profit-sharing basis. In 1967 John Armitage, the co-owner of David's, offered to rent a room in the warden's flat as a private office and bookstore, as the warden was giving up part of the flat.

Despite the obvious progress, financial difficulties continued to dog the Settlement, and they would not be resolved for some years. But 1970 saw the Golden Jubilee, in itself a considerable achievement. A festival was held between 29 April and 16 May, for which a commemorative brochure was produced. A concert was held at St George's church on Saturday, 9 May and featured the Settlement Choir and the Festival Orchestra under its leader Anne Macnaghten and conductor Malcolm Hicks.[44] At the 1970 AGM the President, Mrs Brunt, praised the excellence of the Golden Jubilee:

> [It] demonstrated what can be done when students work together, and would long be remembered for the pleasure it gave. It had been good to see old friends. Perhaps the outstanding meetings of the year had been those of the Second Sunday Club, meetings in friendship that were different to group meetings. Enjoyment came from meeting, talking and remembering.[45]

She hoped more young people would come along to the Settlement, as all interests were catered for, leading to a wide diversity. She believed the new Open University[46] could lead to a revival of culture and she wondered what part the Settlement could play.

The ethos of the Settlement was encapsulated at the 1948 AGM by the newly elected warden, Cedric Davies, who said that he hoped to attract more

21 Student Fellowship float, nd. The Student Fellowship was an important group in the early days of the Settlement; half of the governing body was made up of its members and they had a lot of influence in what classes were taught, as well as how the Settlement was run. There were many pageants in the 1920s and 1930s, largely organised by the Student Fellowship. This one appears to show some of the classes running at the time, such as tennis, but it is impossible to work out what they all are. There is a nice model of the Settlement.

22 Children's game, Jan 1961. Many events were held at the Settlement; this shows children playing 'pass the parcel'. Sadly, there is no information about the event. GCC FGCHM588.189

23 Common room, nd. It shows the fireplace and the 'bar' (which is still used for serving refreshments) and the entrance to the Brunt Room. The people have not been identified.

24 Photograph of Roy Evans taken from a newspaper article about the fortieth anniversary of the Skittles Inn, 1965. GCC LBM4074.15.325

students who might feel diffident about their ability to join in with more advanced students; he hoped to develop the social side and form classes of a more elementary nature. In thanking his predecessor, Miss Richards, for her co-operation, he said:

During the Spring when it was my duty to look through past records of the Settlement, I felt many times that I was reading the story and romance of the development of Letchworth and I felt that when the time came for this meeting I must end my report with my own feeling of gratitude for those who have gone before me. Now-a-days there is a tendency to look forward to the brave new world and at the same time to decry or forget all that has been done in the past. Letchworth, with all its imperfections is only the wonderful town it is – and it is a wonderful town – because of the pioneers who put all their energies into both work and play. Sir Ebenezer Howard, Mr Barry Parker, Mr Pearsall, Mr Charles Ball and hosts of others, many of whom were interested in this Settlement. I feel that here – The Old Skittles Inn turned into a Centre for Adult Education and Recreation – here, is part of the pioneer work started in 1905 and a [sic] made a success in its beginnings by private enterprise (or shall we say individual endeavour). And I think with gratitude of our past Wardens, Mr Dudley, Mr Milliken, Mr Short, Miss Richards and with special affection for Miss Pym and Miss Dewe and all Chairmen, Secretaries and Treasurers and other Officers. And I think it would be wise to think a little on their work and then to look forward, putting our best, as they did, into a great venture of which this work is but part.[47]

Endnotes

1 Garden City Collection, 1959.52.
2 For more on Dudley and other key figures, see chapter 7.
3 See <https://www.wea.org.uk/news-events/blogs/ministry-reconstructions-final-report-adult-education> for more information.
4 Ibid., 2018.21.8.68.
5 The Co-operative Hall was above the shops in Eastcheap and was the venue for many social occasions.
6 Garden City Collection, 2018.21.6.11.
7 Ibid., 2018.21.7.30.
8 Ibid., 2018.21.17.83.
9 Ibid., 2018.21.7.30.
10 This is an interesting insight into those who used the Settlement from the perspective of a working-class child.
11 Elliott, H, and Sanderson, J (co-ordinators), *Letchworth Recollections* (Baldock), 1995, pp. 53–8.
12 Garden City Collection, LS 7C.
13 Ibid., LS 7E. It is unclear exactly what these were.
14 See chapter 8 for more information on the Players.
15 Garden City Collection, 2018.21.13.147. Cockerell was the well-known bookbinder, who taught at the Settlement. His comment about elitism reflects a similar sentiment expressed by Edna Mallett.
16 Ibid., 2018.21.9.42.
17 Ibid., LS 7G.
18 Ibid., 2018.21.15.80.
19 Ibid., 2018.21.15.129.
20 The first civic week was held in 1926, when the Duke of York visited the town. See Miller, M, *Letchworth. The First Garden City*, p. 139.
21 Garden City Collection, 21.18.57, report in *The Citizen*.
22 This was set up by the government for unemployed men, many of whom were ex-miners from South Wales; see Elliott, H, and Sanderson, J (co-ordinators), *Letchworth Recollections* (Baldock), 1995, p. 93.
23 Ibid., 2018.21.13.19 (report in *The Citizen*, 14 November 1930). There is more about the Ascot centre during the second world war later in this chapter.
24 Lloyds moved to Letchworth in 1913 and are still based here; see <http://www.lloydsandco.com/about-us.php>.
25 Ibid., LBM4074.15.
26 Possibly Egerton St John Pettifor Catchpool [*sic*]; see <https://www.oxforddnb.com/view/10.1093/ref:odnb/9780198614128.001.0001/odnb-9780198614128-e-37268?rskey=Mdb19k&result=1>.
27 Garden City Collection, 2018.21.13.119.
28 Reported at the Executive Committee meeting held on 13 May 1931, Garden City Collection, LS 7G.
29 Garden City Collection, 2018.21.9.64.
30 See chapter 7 for more information on Mr and Mrs Higgs.
31 Ibid., re John Short. There is more about Short's army service in chapter 7.
32 There were several in the town and the nearest was probably the one in Bridge Road.
33 Garden City Collection, 2018.21.23.28.
34 The doctor was Marion Cockerell, whose husband was the bookbinder Douglas Cockerell.
35 See chapter 7 for more details.
36 Settlement annual report, 1942/43.
37 It is not clear which town she was talking about.

38 Garden City Collection, LS 7O.

39 Lewis Falk, nephew of Max Herz, who brought the Garden City Embroidery Works to the town in 1907.

40 Garden City Collection, LS 10J.

41 Ibid., LS 5B, 2018.21.52.

42 Ibid., LS 7R.

43 Ibid., LS 5F, 2018.21.56, *The Citizen*, 30 July 1954.

44 Ibid., 2018.21.29.3 & 4.

45 Garden City Collection, LS 7/T.

46 Founded in 1969.

47 Garden City Collection, LS 7S.

Chapter 4

VILLAGE WORK

Work in the villages began almost as soon as the Settlement was founded. At a Council meeting on 9 April 1921, the warden reported on a most successful social at Arlesey and there was also discussion about courses in Hitchin.[1] The following month it was hoped to start a class in Weston and in July the warden reported on a successful meeting in Baldock at which a committee had been formed to take the idea forward.[2] By October, there were six village classes including one at Radwell, and at the 1921 AGM it was reported that of between 250 and 300 students, 100 were in village classes in Baldock, Arlesey, Weston, Radwell and Stotfold.[3] A conference was held on 24 June 1922 where many local organisations agreed to work together to help local villages. One speaker was Miss Hadow,[4] who described the co-operation in other counties:

> Each body is kept fully informed of what others are doing, overlapping and waste of effort are avoided, interchange of lecturers takes place, co-operation in transport leads to economy of expense for all the organisations, and each receives a stimulus by being brought into closer association with others working with the same motives and ideals.[5]

Dudley reported that the conference was unanimously in favour of attempting something similar in Hertfordshire and he was instructed to contact the various county organisations represented, asking them to consider the matter and let him know if they were willing to co-operate in this way. By November the following year there had been requests from Meppershall, Henlow, Ashwell and Weston, and by March 1924 the warden reported on work in Stevenage, Hitchin and the possibility of a new class in Weston. In October he said that there were more classes than before and in larger numbers; there had been seventy-five people at a social in Arlesey and several RAF men from Henlow had joined some of the classes, although it is unclear if this refers to Arlesey or Letchworth. At the 1924 AGM the 100 people attending included students from Arlesey, Baldock, Meppershall, Radwell, Weston, Ashwell and Stevenage.

From as early as September 1922, there was some discussion about co-operating with the Rural Community Council.[6] An issue of *The Worker* on 17 April 1924 said:

> It is good news that the Herts Education Committee has agreed to recommend to the County Council the adoption of the Rural Libraries Scheme... Under this scheme boxes of books will be available for any village in the County that cares to apply to the Central Library for them and that can provide the local machinery for the circulation of the books... Great credit is due to the Rural Community Council (brought into being chiefly through the Letchworth Adult Educational Settlement) which has consistently pressed this scheme upon the County Council.[7]

Six months later, *The Herts Advertiser & St Albans Times* referred to a meeting with the Rural Community Council[8] and by June 1927 there was the possibility of co-operation with the organisation in the provision of village classes.

By November 1925 the warden was giving lectures to teachers at Buntingford on Saturday mornings and there were twenty-five in the class; he was also lecturing to 200 men at the Henlow Aerodrome on 'Modern Novelists', in response to a private invitation.[9] New classes were added all the time; in April 1929 it was hoped to start a class in Graveley and six months later it was reported that Mr Porteous had started work as a staff tutor and was taking classes at Arlesey and Holwell. Edna Mallett, the caretakers' daughter, was rather dismissive of Porteous:

> The young assistant warden, Mr Porteous, whom my parents thought rather silly and improvident (left the lights on all night and didn't lock up) tried to convey the beauty of the nude to my mother, in the cause of art. But she had her sweeping to do, and pointed out that as a former nurse she had plenty of acquaintance with naked bodies, and corpses too, if it came to that![10]

An article by Mary Ibberson, entitled 'The History of a Village Class', was published in *The Educational Settlements Association Bulletin*; it is undated but the journal was the predecessor to *The Common Room* and dates from March 1924.[11] The village is not identified but is quite likely to have been Weston. Ibberson took music classes and described the first term's class of seven or eight women – the village laundress, three teachers, the Vicar's sister, a village housewife or two, and a cook; the cook confided to a friend that the music class was the one thing in the week which she lived for, and that she had taken up the violin. Ibberson said: 'They sang rounds and folk-songs, and listened to informal talks about music and musicians, with a never-failing enthusiasm which repaid the class-leader for her sometimes perilous journeys in an uncertain side-car.' Ibberson described the work in her book:[12]

A most valuable discussion was held in the laundry, where one of the greatest characters of the village discoursed on the past glories when her grandfather played the double-bass in Church, and folk-dances were danced at social gatherings; when young people were courteous to their elders, and not "wild and rude like the present generation!". The laundress felt that a class in country dancing would be a great attraction, and has supported her opinions by faithful attendance through all the vicissitudes of the class.

She talked about a social which was 'a tremendous success' but exhausting for the organisers:

The villagers were quite content to sit round the room and be entertained, especially if the boys were allowed to smoke and keep up an uninterrupted flow of chatter; but at first they had no idea of taking part in their own festivities, or of mixing with those outside their own group… and when, finally, enough dancers were induced to stand up and arrange themselves in two lines [for the 'Sir Roger'], it was found that boys were dancing with boys, and girls with girls!... [A] large number of the village boys confided to a visitor that they always felt 'out of it' at Socials because they could not dance, and felt too rough and ungainly in their thick boots.

This led to a sword-dance class for boys only being formed and Ibberson continued with a full description of the various events. Although the article is undated, she refers to classes in the spring and summer of 1923. She concluded by saying that her account could not give an adequate idea of the real results of three winters of adult education in the village:

Watch the boys after their day's ploughing or carting, learning to use brain and body simultaneously in the strenuous and intricate mazes of their sword-dance, and see what pride and added self-respect their achievement gives them. They bring rubber shoes, wear clean collars, brush their hair, and even occasionally pluck up courage to ask an elegant young woman from a different social group… to dance with them! See with what abandon that elderly lady who has 'bad legs', and certainly bad luck in life, 'sings herself away to realms of endless bliss', as a sympathetic onlooker once remarked! Another middle-aged lady has bought a pair of rubber shoes, and, being light-footed, hopes soon to work her way into the country house team. She has only recently come out of the asylum, to which she had been driven by melancholia induced by loneliness and worry. Why does that woman at the back walk two miles to the school regularly and two miles back? She has never taken her hat off or been known to dance a step or sing a note, but we should all miss her if she did not come… An outsider would find the class rough enough, but words cannot express the leader's pride when a boy, having to leave early, comes up to excuse himself, and say good-night, or when others undertake the responsibility of putting the forms away each week. No one but she can appreciate how friendliness has triumphed over snobbishness, when a certain superior young woman dances with a rough hobbledehoy ploughboy.

There was great excitement in 1930 when students built a 'wireless', so that they could listen to BBC lectures:

Wireless at Settlement

A wireless set made largely by members of the electricity and magnetism class has recently been added to the equipment of the Settlement. The set was intended chiefly for village work, and has already been used at Hinxworth with great success. This term the set will be working on Tuesday and Friday evenings at the Settlement at 8 and 8.30 pm respectively for psychology and bio-chemistry talks.[13]

There is an interesting article in the Settlement's in-house magazine, dated 21 June 1930 and entitled 'How the radio came to Hinxworth' by Agnes Danby. It describes the warden and Agnes taking the radio set from the Settlement to Hinxworth village hall so that the people there could hear a lecture from the BBC.[14]

The annual conference of the Educational Settlements Association in 1930 discussed education in rural areas, describing it as 'yet in its infancy, but it is growing and it is well to remember that some of the very earliest pioneer work was done by the Letchworth Settlement under the wardenship of Mr James Dudley...'[15] The *Beds & Herts Pictorial* reported on the summer fair and that William Wallace Kincaid had promised a substantial sum of money, enough to pay for a rural tutor for the autumn and spring terms 1930/31.[16] This was referred to at the 1932 AGM:

Through the generosity of Mr Kincaid and others, the Settlement work in the villages had made progress. Classes had been held in the following villages, Arlesey, Ashwell, Hinxworth, Newnham, Graveley, Clothall, Kimpton, Langford and Sandon. By giving facilities for wood carving and carpentering they had tried to do something for the unemployed. Up to the present there had not been the response hoped for, but those who had attended at the beginning were keen workers and had obtained intermittent work.[17]

In February 1931 Bernard Ellis had given six lectures at Hinxworth and there had been a request for more, but it was difficult for him to get there.[18] As well as the Arlesey Dramatic Class, which was reported as giving excellent performances, a drama group started in Graveley; it produced *Arms and the Man*, which was apparently a great success.[19] In January 1932 new classes started at Newnham and Langford, and it was hoped to start one at Clothall; three years later Rushden and Walkern joined the list.

A conference on rural adult education was held at the Settlement in April 1932, which got a lot of press coverage. One report described Douglas Cockerell's remarks that adult education in the village should not only be vocational, but cultural, and he drew attention to some of the village classes: 'drama, music, dancing, history, and the League of Nations'. Clothall was having a talk on 'The Present Crisis' and Arlesey was 'taking on such a big thing as "The Reconstruction of Europe"...'[20] George Bernard Shaw paid a 'quite unexpected visit' on the Saturday afternoon:[21]

> At his session Mr Bernard Shaw, who had been invited as a member of the Hertfordshire Society,[22] unexpectedly put in an appearance and asked a few questions... Mr Bernard Shaw, intervening at question time, asked what proportion of village workers would attend classes; was it only a small group of 'intelligentsia'? Had the lecturers ever tried the method of saying 'Here I am, a very intellectual man, ask me questions on any subject you like and I will try to answer them'?[23]

Shaw also said: 'They [the tutors] had talked about sending the farm workers to the university for a year – had they thought about sending the university student to the farm for a year?'[24]

25   George Bernard Shaw at a conference on rural education, 1932. GCC 2018.21.14.130 Shaw is second from the left in the back row; Ruth Pym is on the far left in the front row and Barry Parker is next to her; James Dudley is at the far right of the front row.

Mrs Wheeler said that, as far as she remembered, the only reason they could expect grants from the Educational Settlements Association was on the strength of the village work which they undertook, adding that 'The Settlement had originally been started in Letchworth because it was situated in a very advantageous position for village work'. This is the first time that this appears to have been spelt out, but it does reinforce the importance of the village work from the very start of the Settlement. The chairman went on to say:

> ...that the ESA would look at Letchworth very much askance if they dropped the village work. Mr Bishop (Arlesey) spoke of the Settlement's efforts in Arlesey, saying that they could not induce the villagers to come into the class, for what reason they did not know. Mr Skinner remarked that the expense incurred in the village work was something like £70, and in comparison with the number of village students they might as well have given them a pound each and got them to come into Letchworth. It was remarked that there was no guarantee in the event of such a system that the villagers, having had their fares paid into Letchworth, would come to the Settlement and that they might go to the pictures.[25]

An undated document, thought to be from the 1930s, lists the village classes.[26] Most of them were for music, dancing and drama. Seven weeks had been spent on a survey, made in conjunction with the Hertfordshire Society: 'The work [on the survey] is of necessity slow, and obstacles and setbacks many, but it is hoped that by the end of the year the extra-mural work of the Settlement will be of increased value to the rural areas'. A second report, from about the same time, reported on the work of Mr N G Luker, who had taught the Newnham history class. He had visited twenty-three villages and transport was provided by Mr D Capper, secretary of the Hertfordshire Society, who was able to introduce school head teachers and clergy in the villages to Mr Luker. Mr Luker found some pessimism in the more isolated villages regarding the intelligence and interest of their local people. Despite this, classes had started in three of them and two others were due to start. He quoted some of the local worthies, including a lady involved with the local WI, who apparently said: 'Mr Luker has brought in just the very men I wanted to help, young fellows of 18–23 who otherwise spend the evenings standing round the sign post at the corner'.[27] This document refers to the Arlesey class, saying: 'the class consists of 10 very serious and intelligent men, who not only discuss but write papers on their work'. In contrast to the general positivity, Hilda Richardson, the secretary of the Arlesey Dramatic Group, said that they had only received two visits from a tutor [in 1935] and 'no subscription will be forthcoming'.[28]

One of the problems with the village classes was, of course, transport. In June 1933 a car was bought for village lecturers to use. As a result of lectures at Sandon, the class, under the leadership of Mr Westell,[29] was carrying out excavations 'with interesting results'. Mr Westell was welcomed to the Council as a new representative of the Naturalists' Society.[30] New classes continued to be added; in December 1936 additions were reported in Wallington, as well as classes in villages which had featured before. The second world war curtailed activity, however, mainly due to the inability to buy petrol. The 1939/40 annual report said:

> It is true to say that all educational bodies found village work very difficult last winter. Apart from the question of black-out and accommodation, it was generally found that the kind of village people who had previously attended our classes were the very people who were the first to volunteer for civilian defence and first aid duties. Nevertheless two drama groups were taken by the Warden at Holwell and a spirited production of 'St Simeon Stylites' by F Sladen-Smith was given in the early spring. Besides this the Warden arranged and gave a series of lectures in the neighbouring villages on 'The Spirit of France' – a study of the literature of our ally.[31]

The 1940/41 annual report said that, in addition to the difficulties mentioned a year earlier, men were being called up, and a relatively large number of both men and women were working for the Auxiliary Fire Service and as air-raid wardens.[32] In April 1941 it was reported that village classes were practically at a standstill, but the following November the warden reported that he was trying to re-start them and to get petrol to enable this, but there is no information about how successful he was. The annual reports for 1942/43 and 1943/44 have no references to the village classes but in March 1946 the Executive Committee discussed resuming them; the warden, Miss Richards, had written to a number of villages but only the Rector of Ashwell had replied, asking for lectures on international affairs.

The next meeting, in April, was attended by Mr Prideaux, Director of Further Education for the County Council, and he referred to the 1944 Education Act. Among other provisions, this Act made local education authorities responsible for securing adequate further education provision, including 'leisure-time occupation, and such organised cultural training and recreative activities as are suited to their requirements, for any persons over compulsory school age who are able and willing to profit by the facilities provided for that purpose'.[33] Mr Prideaux believed that there were two ways of dealing with village education: responding to a demand which had already been experienced and provoking such a demand where it was latent. The Settlement agreed to support him in every way; he would compile a panel of people who would be willing to go out into the villages and Miss Richards would do the same.[34] It seems, however, that the curtailment of village classes during the war, together with the impact of the 1944 Act, effectively stopped the Settlement providing them any longer: the classes in Bedfordshire became the responsibility of Bedfordshire County Council.

Some of the most memorable work in the villages concerned the Rural Music School. This was started by Mary Ibberson while she was sub-warden of the Settlement. She was passionate about taking music into villages and tells a story about an attempt to make good teaching available to amateurs of all ages, not in the large centres of professional music but in country towns and villages. It was intended at first for adults only. When the first one started, she said: 'social and educational conditions in the villages were very different from those of today, but the desire for music and music-making was clearly present in many country people'. [35]

It appears that Letchworth was unusual in its provision of village classes and sowed the seeds for many of them to continue after the Settlement's involvement ended. The number of classes, the range of subjects and the dedication of tutors and students were impressive.

Endnotes

1   Garden City Collection, LS 7A.
2   Hitchin and Baldock were towns rather than villages, but the Settlement had a presence there as well as in the villages.
3   Ibid., 2018.21.1.30.
4   Presumably Grace Hadow, OBE, principal of St John's College Oxford and Vice Chair of the National Federation of Women's Institutes.
5   Garden City Collection, 2018.21.1.41.
6   Rural Community Councils were founded between the two world wars but few of them have survived. It is difficult to find information about the Hertfordshire RCC; it appears to have become known as Community Development Action, <https://www.cdaherts.org.uk/hertfordshires-rural-conference-2016/?doing_wp_cron=1581507957.4613869190216064453125>.
7   Garden City Collection 2018.21.2.88.
8   Ibid., 2018.21.1.60.
9   Ibid., LS 7D.
10   See chapter 3 for a long quote from Edna Mallett, Elliott, H and Sanderson, J (co-ordinators), *Letchworth Recollections* (Baldock), 1995.
11   Garden City Collection, 2018.21.22.48; information from Mark Freeman on date.
12   Ibberson, M, *For joy that we are here. Rural Music Schools 1929–1950* (London), 1977.
13   Garden City Collection, 2018.21.12.61; *The Citizen*, 2 May 1930.
14   Ibid., 201.21.8.68.
15   Ibid., 2018.21.8.76.
16   Ibid., 2018.21.13.127.
17   Ibid., 2018.21.14.123, report from *The Citizen*.
18   Ibid., LS 7I.
19   Ibid., LS 7G.
20   Ibid., 2018.21.14.62, *Advertiser*, 5 May 1932.
21   Ibid., 2018.21.14.80.
22   The Hertfordshire Society was an amalgamation of the Hertfordshire Rural Community Council and the local branch of the Council for the Protection of Rural England.
23   Garden City Collection, 2018.21.14.62.
24   Ibid., 2018.21.14.71.
25   Ibid., 2018.21.14.83.
26   Ibid., 2018.21.22.29.
27   Ibid., 2018.21.22.48.
28   Ibid., 2018.21.22.12.
29   W Percival Westell was the first curator of Letchworth Museum & Art Gallery; see <https://en.wikipedia.org/wiki/Letchworth_Museum_%26_Art_Gallery>.
30   Garden City Collection, LS 7I.
31   Settlement annual report, 1939/40. The minimum school leaving age was raised to 15 under the Act.
32   Settlement annual report, 1940/41.
33   Kelly, T, *A History of Adult Education in Great Britain* (Liverpool), 1992, p. 337.
34   Garden City Collection, LS 7O.
35   Ibberson, p. 1.

Chapter 5
CONSOLIDATION

T he next fifty years, from 1971 to 2020, saw changes and developments, with new buildings and activities.[1] Arguably, the most significant event came in 1995 when the then Letchworth Garden City Corporation accepted the building as a gift and leased it back to the Settlement (see pp. 63–4). We are reliant on the minutes and annual reports for most of what we know about this period, but of course there are also the personal memories of a number of people who were associated with the Settlement at the time and are still alive. A key figure is the longest-serving warden, Roy Evans, who was in post from 1963 to 2001.[2]

Financial matters

Finance was a constant worry and there are frequent references to it. In February 1972, for example, there was a long discussion about fund-raising, and at the 1972 AGM the warden reported that the Settlement was still in a hazardous financial position. In May 1975 fees were to rise by twenty per cent; the membership fee was increased to £3, and to £1 for senior citizens. Various fund-raising suggestions were made, in order to run the building satisfactorily and to buy extra equipment. It was announced in May 1984 that the government had withdrawn its £18,000 grant-aid from the Educational Centres Association, which the Association used to support the remaining settlements; letters were sent to various MPs to protest. However, at the 1985 AGM the treasurer compared the finances with those of 1951/52, when Brian Groombridge was the warden, and said that the Settlement was in a very healthy position.

The Settlement has received a number of legacies over the years, most of them quite small, but some more substantial. Memorial funds have also occasionally been set up in memory of people who had supported the Settlement. In March 1985 just over £9,000 was received from the estate of the late Mayblossom Li; she was described as late of Rosehill Hospital[3] and formerly of Wyvenhoe, 22 Sollershott West. She died on 9 September 1984, aged 98 and an eighth of her estate was left to the Settlement. In February 1983, after the death of Mr K Coram, his widow offered unspecified gifts to the Settlement in his memory. Ken Spinks died in April 1986 and the Settlement received £250 in his will. Dr Moreton gave £1,000 in 2003/4 and the same sum two years later. In June 2004 the Friends of Maryland College donated £250, as the college had closed.[4] In September 2005 it was reported that donations of about £600 had been received from Mrs Lupton's funeral; Mrs Lupton had been a supporter of the Settlement for many years. In May 2007, the Settlement received £5,000 from the estate of Dennis Chadwick. The most significant donation in recent years was from the estate of Daphne Sutcliffe, which ultimately amounted to £23,000 and was received in 2016.[5]

The death of Miles Tabor was reported at the 1983 AGM; he had acted as honorary solicitor to the Settlement;[6] the following June it was stated that a projector had been bought from the Miles Tabor memorial fund. The sudden and unexpected death of the chairman, Dick Trollope, was announced in March 2001 and a memorial fund (of £1,210) was partly used to buy new crockery and cutlery. The Diana Evans memorial fund was used to buy a dishwasher. The death of Shirley Osborne was announced in January 2001 and it was decided to install a bench in her memory, which is still there; her husband Brian, now also deceased, did a lot of work in the garden from 2002.

Administration

The administrative structure of the Settlement changed over time but for much of its existence it was run by a Council and a Management Committee, whose responsibilities overlapped. The Council was formally abolished at the 2008 AGM and the governing body is now known as the Management Committee and all its members are trustees. With Dick Trollope's death, the Settlement was left without a chair until Mrs Pat Ellis stepped forward. She galvanised action on many fronts, including significant works in the hall and the refurbishment of the stage and theatre facilities. She was succeeded by Mrs Carola Garvie, who took over as chair in 2008. She led the organisation through a period of increasing activity, the negotiation of a new lease for the building and extended car parking. Mrs Garvie was succeeded in 2014 by Mrs Pam Burn, who remains chair in 2020. At the time of writing, the Settlement is financially stable after a number of years of careful stewardship, most notably under that of John Bird; after ten years as treasurer, he became president, a post he still holds today. His wisdom and financial acuity have been of enormous benefit.

The building

Because of its age, the former Skittles Inn has been subject to perennial problems. The 1972/73 annual report describes serious issues with the building: emergency repairs to the leaking hot-water cylinder were required and more of the roof needed to be patched. In the 1973/74 annual report the warden described the year as remarkable, but not in a good way; he referred to 'savage' increases in the price of oil as well as power restrictions. The early part of 1974 became known as 'the three-day week', when businesses faced severe constraints on their use of electricity, the miners went on strike and petrol coupons were issued (but never used) in anticipation of a shortage of supplies.[7]

At the 1974 AGM the Corporation was thanked for tables, a vacuum cleaner, work on the car park and help in paying off the balance of the gas-conversion debt;[8] it had given £400 for the last item. The County Council gave a grant of £500, plus £330 for decorating the hall and towards the warden's salary; the District Council gave a grant of £150. Two new classrooms were created, designed by Hugh Bidwell, one of which was to be used for crafts. All the rooms were renamed: the lecture room became the Lily and Donald Brunt Room, Room 1 the Ken and Gwen Spinks Room and Room 2 the John and Jo Cruse Room. In the event, these names were shortened to just the surnames and still bear them today. The new extensions were officially opened on 19 September 1975 and increased the accommodation by a third. In May 1982 there was discussion about an extension above the Spinks and Cruse rooms, but this did not happen.

The warden ended his tenancy of the flat on 17 March 1975 and he and his family moved out the same month; it was not re-let and became two teaching rooms, one named the Williams Room, after Joan Williams, former president. In September 1977 water flooded into the hall, due to inadequate drainage, and there was a leak in the hall roof. The building was listed with English Heritage (now known as Historic England) as grade II on 7 September 1979, which meant that any future alterations would need prior approval.

In 1983–84 the biggest project was implementing the changes required by the Fire Officer.[9] Double-glazing was installed in the Cruse and Spinks rooms the following year, which was timely as it was another bad winter. By the 1986 AGM, the building was declared to be in a very good standard of repair and decoration. The following year an energy working party was established and it sought grant-aid for a new boiler.[10] In 1991 Thames TV used the Settlement for a crime-prevention film. In the same year 'Operation Clean Up' involved twenty volunteers who 'toiled away in the grounds'; great quantities of hedge were thinned, the common room was decorated and improvements made to the Cruse and Spinks rooms.[11] A 'no smoking' ban was first discussed in March 1988 but was not implemented until 1996.

In March 1992 it was decided to accept Howes and Boughton's quotation of £10,720 for work to the roof above the Cruse and Spinks rooms, and the covered way and entrance hall foyer. In November 1993 it was reported that the Board of Letchworth Corporation had agreed in principle to take over responsibility for external maintenance of the buildings, which would require a change in the lease, and the following March it was noted that the Corporation would re-roof the original Settlement building. At the 1994 AGM Miss Williams commented that the Settlement used to be fairly stable but the previous three years 'had seen many crises', among them a lack of subsidy, a reduction in the warden's hours, and trustee and lease problems. According to those who were involved at the time, this period was the Settlement's bleakest hour and without the help of the Corporation it would have ceased to exist. There were many maintenance problems which the Settlement could not afford to address and decreasing funding, which led to a severe lack of confidence on the part of both students and trustees. Becoming a trustee was seen as something of a poisoned chalice.[12]

An application for lottery funding in 1996 was refused because it related to maintenance. The following year the Settlement, together with the Heritage Foundation (which succeeded the Corporation in 1995), applied for another grant, for several different pieces of work: the replacement of asbestos in the hall and theatre roof, the removal of an asbestos lining above the stage, upgrading of windows, lighting, sound system and CCTV, the replacement of tiles in the main passageway and outdoor stoep area, and restoration works to the main building, including windows, settles, fireplaces and decorative schemes.[13] The sum asked for was £30,000 but this was also refused, because a criterion was that buildings needed to be in urgent need of repair. The Heritage Foundation was advised and promised continuing support, dependent on matching funds being available.

In 1999 the telephone cable snapped, and there was no phone access for over a month, something that is unimaginable today. In March 1999 John Elson discussed the proposed extension to the stage; it was suggested that this should be a flap, to a depth of three feet, which would not damage the floor. The estimated cost of about £1,000 would be borne by the Settlement Players, and the extension was to be in memory of Noel Ripley, who had been involved with the Players for many years and wrote one of its online histories.[14] In May 1999 the Heritage Foundation had approved a grant of £20,000 (half the expected cost) for the renovations required, especially to the kitchen. In 2000 the building was sympathetically renovated and enhanced, providing a modern kitchen, new classrooms and a toilet for the disabled.[15]

In 2005 the inglenook in the Brunt Room was restored and a new classroom, known as the Garden Room, provided on the ground floor by turning two small storage rooms into a new space. They had been used by the Settlement Players, who were compensated with better facilities and an extension to the stage. The architect was Nigel Carrick and he raised about £60,000 for the work.[16] The bulk of this, £45,000, came in the form of a grant from WREN (Waste Recycling Environmental), which awards grants to community projects.[17] In

October 2007 it was stated that the extra work in the hall would cost about £63,000, most of which was for an extension to the stage. In September 2014 there was a proposal for a new arts-and-crafts building, which would have meant demolishing the Cruse and Spinks rooms. Sadly, the Settlement had to accept that it could not afford the loss of income whilst the old craft block was rebuilt, and so the project was shelved.

Another ongoing issue was with the car park, which was not large enough to accommodate all the users at any one time. In November 1985 discussions began with Network Rail, the owners of the adjacent land, about extending it. This was completed in 2006, by using land leased for thirty years on a peppercorn rent; £30,000 was needed for work before the additional space could be brought into use. A further offer of more land was negotiated with Network Rail in October 2014, but after quotations in excess of £40,000 were received to clear and convert the rough ground to provide car parking sufficient for only seventeen cars, the Management Committee decided not to proceed. It is interesting to note that in the early days some car park spaces were leased to the Salvation Army, which adjoins the Settlement, and a local car-dealer.

Security

There have been perennial security problems and more than one break-in. In April 1992 the door to the stage was smashed and the Settlement Players lost about £600 worth of equipment. There was another burglary in August 1992; this time a tape recorder, calculator, answerphone, tools and other items were stolen. A window in the ladies' downstairs cloakroom had been broken to afford entry and padlocks on the cashboxes had been smashed. The following month Mr Elson and Mr Fyfe were warmly thanked for putting metal bars on the windows. In June 1996 there was another break-in and again on the night of 10/11 August 1998; a kitchen window was broken and cash stolen from the canteen cupboard and office. In September 2002 someone was sleeping rough outside the building; he had used the outside sink as a lavatory and broken into the Cruse and Spinks rooms. In March 2010 a quote for replacing lead stolen from the roof was received and the following month the Crime Prevention Officer of Hertfordshire Police advised that video-camera surveillance be installed.

Transfer of the building to Letchworth Corporation

The original ground lease, between the Skittles Inn and First Garden City Ltd, was dated 27 September 1906; it was for ninety-nine years, expiring in 2005, and at a nominal rent. As described in chapter 2, the Settlement had purchased the building in 1925. In November 1975 Letchworth Corporation agreed to an alteration in the lease allowing alcohol to be sold, subject to the appropriate licence being obtained. By the early 1990s there was deep anxiety about the condition of the building, as described above. In March 1992 there was a meeting with the solicitors and it appeared that the 1925 deed was missing; the warden wrote to the Charity Commissioners to see if they had a copy but this drew a blank. It had become apparent that there were no remaining trustees; the lease was held by the relatives of the last one to die, Margaret Harvey, leaving a vacuum. It was necessary to appoint new trustees and when this had been done it would be desirable to discuss the renewal of the lease.

At the Management Committee meeting on 16 May 1994, a letter was read from Mr J M Hillson of the Corporation, outlining proposals for a new lease. It was proposed that the Settlement surrender the existing one and the Corporation would offer a new ten-year lease starting the same day. In addition, the Corporation would take over liabilities for all the structural external repairs to the building. Once it was made clear that the trustees' duties under the new lease were less onerous, it was possible to find suitable people. By the 1994 AGM a new trust deed had been formally drawn up and approved by the Council. The four new trustees were Mrs Lesley Geaney (North Herts College), Mr William Armitage (Letchworth Civic Trust), Mr Michael E Richardson (University of Cambridge Board of Continuing Education) and Mrs Ann Crook (Education 2000). The rent was £50 a year, and there was an option to renew the lease for a further ten years. Two years later, it was stated that, with the signing of the new lease, the value of the leasehold buildings (£7,971 the previous year) had been written off against a contingency fund.

After several meetings and discussions about the need to settle the long-term future of the Settlement, a new lease was agreed with the Heritage Foundation in 2013 and signed two years later. It was for a period of fifty years, on payment of a peppercorn rent until 2036, after which the rental would be subject to renegotiation according to an agreed, but complex formula. The Foundation also carried out a full external redecoration and various other works, but thereafter the Settlement was to be responsible for all repairs and maintenance.

Staffing issues

In February 1969, what became known as the Russell Committee was set up by the Secretary of State, chaired by Sir Lionel Russell, CBE. Its terms of reference were to assess the need for and to review the provision of non-vocational adult education in England and Wales; to consider the appropriateness of existing educational policies; and to make recommendations with a view to obtaining the most effective and economical deployment of available resources to enable adult education to make its proper contribution to the national system of education. The report was published in March 1973 and in September 1973 was discussed at some length.[18] The Settlement Council was clearly nervous about the implications for the Settlement's future. In March 1978 it was reported that

Plate 1   Painting by C J Fox, in oils, nd. An attractive image of the Skittles Inn before the Settlement occupied the building. GCC ref 461

Plate 2   Portrait of James Dudley, warden from 1920 to 1927, by Rev A J Bamford.

Plate 3   View of the Settlement common room by Elsie Lamb, 1940s–50s. North Herts Museum.

Plate 4   Portrait of Ruth Pym, in Green Room. It was commissioned by the chairman, Lewis Falk, but the artist is not known.

Plate 5   Ruth Pym tea trolley, created as a memorial to her and currently used by the Settlement Players as a props store.

Plate 6   Colourised photograph of common room, at the Settlement.

Plate 7   Portrait of William Wallace Kincaid, whose legacy paid for the hall named after him; currently in storage at the Settlement. The artist is unknown.

Plate 8   Roy Evans at the Skittles Inn centenary exhibition in 2007.

Plate 9   Wall hanging, designed by Dr Schofield, in Kincaid Hall, 2003.

Daily Diary

SC Short Course

MONDAY

Morning

Fictional Elegies 1	25
Fictional Elegies 2	31
Get Writing for All SC	23
Adventures in Watercolours	8
Upholstery	11
LALG	41
Brush Up Your Latin SC	32
A Journey Through Sufi Voices SC	32
Great Advances in Physics	27
Experiments Which Changed the Course of Science	32
Art and Empire: British Art and the World in the 19th Century	37
Spanish – Beginners	20
Patchwork and Quilting	10

Afternoon

Caligari's Children: 100 Years of Gothic Cinema	25
Getting Dressed: A History of Clothes	31
Night Moves: An Introduction to Neo-noir Cinema SC	14
The First Artists SC	37
Roman Britain Art & Society SC	26
Medieval Britain Art and Society SC	31
Early English Art and Architecture SC	31
Botanical Art: Luscious Leaves and All Things Green SC	13
Botanical Art: Seedheads from the Garden SC	14
Chinese Brush Painting – Landscape SC	14
Chinese Brush Painting – Insects and Animals SC	14
Botanical Art: Flowers, Fruit and Vegetables SC	14
Portraits Using Coloured Pencils SC	15

Evening

Creative Beginnings SC	31
Basic Bookmaking SC	18
Woven Tapestry for Beginners SC	16
Upholstery	11
Simply Sewing	10
German Beginners Plus	22
French Beginners	19
First Garden City Ladies Group	42
Jane Austen's Northanger Abbey SC	27
Mrs Dalloway by Virginia Woolf SC	27
A Novel by Hilary Mantel SC	32
Reader I Married Him: A Closer Look at Jane Eyre by Charlotte Brontë SC	33
The Enchanted April by Elizabeth von Arnim SC	37
Script Reading Shakespeare: A Midsummer Night's Dream SC	37
Remembering The Beatles SC	27

TUESDAY

Morning

50+ Exercise to Music	24
Keep Fit	24
Britain and the Ottoman Empire from Elizabeth 1 to Gallipoli SC	26
Classical Mythology: A Literary and Visual Tour through the Classical Authors SC	26
Upholstery	11
Abstract Painting	8
Russian – Beginners	22
Settlement Players	41
Dance Steps Academy	42
Table Tennis	41
Letchworth & Hitchin Chess Club	41
Letchworth Garden City Society	42

Evening

Spanish – Beginners	20
Still Life & Life Drawing	8
Knitting for Beginners SC	17
Crochet for Beginners SC	17
Knitting for Improvers SC	17
Friends and Relief: Quaker Engagement in Europe SC	28
The Roaring 20s: A Decade in Music SC	33
Machine Embroidery	10
Drawing for Beginners & All SC	15
Simply Sewing: A Focus on Technique SC	16
Acrylic Painting SC	15
Chinese Brush Painting – Flower Compositions SC	15

Crochet for Improvers SC	17
Letchworth Art Society	40
Letchworth Natural History Society	42
Dance Steps Academy	42

WEDNESDAY

Morning

Cake Decorating & Sugarcraft SC	12
Expressive Watercolours	8
French – Improvers 2	19
French – Advanced Conversation	19
Get Writing for All SC	23
In and Out of the Workhouse	28
Oxygen, the Breath of Life SC	28
The First Men on the Moon and the advent of the First Re-Useable Spacecraft SC	34
Women with Wings: Remarkable Aviatrix SC	34
Water, Water Everywhere: The Story of the Fens	38
Britain Since 1800: Origins of the Present Crisis	33
Artists in Cornwall SC	33
Special Effects in the Movies SC	34
Walking with History Part 4 SC	38
Cut Flowers: Autumn SC	13
Cut Flowers: Spring SC	13
Cut Flowers: Summer SC	13
Daytime Art Club	40

Afternoon

Life Drawing	9
German – Beginners	22
Basic Spanish for Tourists	21
Spanish – Discussion Group	21
Spanish – Intermediate	21
French – Advanced Conversation	19
Silver Jewellery Making SC	18
Watercolour Toolbox for Beginners SC	16
Elizabethan Gardens & Shakespeare's Flowers	28
Introduction to Tablet Computers SC	34
Managing Photos on a Tablet Computer SC	35
Making Friends with Windows 10 SC	36

THURSDAY

Morning

25 Club	43
26 Club	43
French – Intermediate 3	19
French – Beginners Plus	20
Sugarcraft: Private Tutored Group	12
Textile Masterclass	11
Creative Stitchery	11
Get Writing for All SC	23
Buildings in England and Their Functions: Schools, Sports and Utilities	29
History of the English Cottage Garden	35
Moving Beyond Point and Shoot – Cameras, not Guns! SC	29
Photography – Beyond the Basics SC	29

Afternoon

Textile Masterclass	11
Creative Stitchery	11
French Improvers 3	20
Oil Painting	9
India: The British Raj 1857-1947	29
Gilbert and Sullivan: Their Times and Tunes	36
Four Quartets by T.S. Eliot SC	30
Caspar David Friedrich SC	30
The Problem of Evil SC	30
J.M.W.Turner SC	35
Mary Magdalene SC	35
Paul Cezanne SC	39

Evening

Wired and Unwired Sugar Flowers for all Occasions	12
Introduction to Glass Fusing SC	18

Turning the Titans of Computing SC	38
Daytime Art Club	40

FRIDAY

Morning

Art of the Landscape	9
Cut Flowers for All	12
Lipreading	25
Success and Scandal in 20th Century Medicine	30
An Introduction into the History of Film Music	36
Famous Russian Women in History and Culture	36
Criminal Psychology	30
Gender and Relationships	36
Freud	11
Writing Fiction and Getting Published	23

Evening

RSPB	43
LALG Wine Appreciation Group	35
LALG Wine Discovery Group	42
Letchworth Recorded Music Society	42
'Bobdun Along'	40

Acrylic Painting SC	15
Art of the Landscape SC	16
Hatha Yoga	24
Poetry ID Group	43
Spinners and Weavers	43
Camera Club	43
Dance Steps Academy	42

Evening

Life Drawing	9
Patchwork and Quilting	10
Simply Sewing	10
Spanish – Improvers	21
Spanish – Intermediate	21
Dance Steps Academy	42
Settlement Players	41

SATURDAY

Watercolour Toolbox – Improvers	10
Dance Steps Academy	42
HUE	40

SUNDAY

Settlement Players	41
Letchworth Sinfonia	42

Rooms are available for hire.

Please enquire in the office.

Term Dates 2019-2020

Autumn
Monday 2 September 2019 (office open normal hours)
Monday 9 September 2019 (Autumn Term starts)

Half-term
Monday 28 October to Friday 1 November 2019

Christmas closure
Monday 16 December 2019 (from 2.00pm) to Wednesday 1 January 2020

Spring
Thursday 2 January 2020 (office open normal hours)
Monday 6 January 2020 (Spring Term starts)

Half-term
Monday 17 February to Friday 21 February 2020

Spring Term end
Friday 3 April 2020 (at 10.00pm)

Easter Break
Monday 6 April to Friday 10 April 2020 (open irregular hours for workshops and hirings)

Easter closure
Friday 10 April to Sunday 19 April 2020

Summer
Monday 20 April 2020 (Summer Term starts)
Monday 4 May 2020 (closed for Bank Holiday)
Monday 25 May 2020 (closed for Bank Holiday)

Half-term
Monday 25 May to Friday 29 May 2020

Summer closure
Saturday 18 July to Sunday 9 August 2020

Please check the individual class details as they may vary from those above.

Plate 10   List of classes from 2019/20 brochure.

the warden was now officially within the Department of Adult Education at North Herts College and seconded full-time to the Settlement; in May 1982 his hours were reduced to thirty per week. At the 1983 AGM it was reported that Hertfordshire County Council paid the warden's salary and North Herts District Council contributed £200 towards it. In January 1986 Roy Evans was co-opted onto the Board of Extra-Mural Studies at Cambridge University; Mrs Joan Cave was appointed as administrative assistant in November 1984.

In 1986 the warden reported that there were more university courses but fewer North Herts College ones. For many years, courses had been put on by Cambridge University and local colleges, as well as by individuals; the first two attracted grant-aid.[19] In June 1989 the chair said that she had written to Mr P Brown, principal of North Herts College, regarding the forthcoming merger of that institution with Stevenage College and had been told that it would not affect the Settlement. At the Council meeting on 17 June 1991 the warden gave a summary of the recent White Paper on education and training for the twenty-first century.[20] It seemed that vocational education for young people would be at the expense of non-vocational courses. As this would affect many of the local college courses held at the Settlement, members were asked to write to their MP. The white paper was also discussed at the 1991 AGM. The Management Committee meeting on 22 January 1992 was attended by Mr R Gochin, who had succeeded Mr Brown as principal of North Herts College, and Mr L Hawke, head of the Department of Adult Education at the college. Mr Gochin spoke about the reorganisation of the College and how it might affect the Settlement; he added that the warden's position would be safeguarded for the foreseeable future. By March 1992 North Herts College courses required a minimum of fourteen enrolments and funding was taken out of local authority control from April 1993. In May 1992 Miss Williams said that the warden had been re-appointed by North Herts College, with a job description of 'Programme Administrator' of local education authority classes. The College was told of all the work that the warden did in addition to organising the programme, such as day schools, supervising staff, maintenance problems, lettings, Settlement courses and so on. The warden pointed out that his successor would be paid for less than thirty-seven hours.

By the end of 1993 there was no longer a full-time warden, due solely to cuts in funding from central government. North Herts College had funded the post for twenty years, 'and for those years The Settlement was grateful'. The College had affirmed that it was committed to funding a part-time administrator; Mr Evans had taken early retirement and had accepted the post of part-time administrator on an annual contract basis and was working for twenty-seven and a half hours a week. In October 1995, as Mr Evans was no longer employed by North Herts College, Mr Hawke suggested that, on presentation of an invoice, the College would pay the Settlement for running its courses. Mr

Evans would be self-employed and paid quarterly. The 1996 AGM reported that Roy Evans was now working for twenty-five hours a week. There were ongoing discussions with North Herts College and the Management Committee felt that not all tutors would wish to become self-employed. In October 1998 the Settlement was looking to develop as a centre of excellence in local studies, archaeology and field archaeology, and social studies. The year 1999 was a difficult one academically: courses sponsored by North Herts College had dwindled, but there was a strong programme of university-sponsored courses. There would be no fee from North Herts College that year, 'Since North Hertfordshire College has ceased to have any courses at the Settlement...'

In April 2000 Roy Evans resigned, saying that he wished to retire at the end of the calendar year. In November, he suggested 20 January 2001 as his official retiring date. In March 2001 it was noted that he had received 'a good send-off' and he was elected as a vice president at the following AGM. He continued to be involved with the Settlement, and is to this day. One of the things he organised, beginning in the early 1980s, was a visits programme; members travelled by coach to various venues around the country to see plays, concerts and exhibitions of many kinds. The programme was very popular, but with the advent of streaming of live performances, attendances gradually fell away, and the last visit to Stratford (to see *Don Quixote*) took place in 2016. Roy was pleased to note in September 2010 that the staff at Buckingham Palace 'commented on our professional approach and superb organisation at our recent visit to the house and gardens'.[21]

There were thirty responses to the advertisement for Roy's successor and five people were interviewed. The post was offered to Mrs Julie Irving, who accepted; she was to be self-employed and to be called 'Manager'.[22] She remained in post until January 2003; advertisements for a replacement were placed in *The Comet* and the *Cambridge Evening News* and Sarah Carrick was appointed the following month. In September 2007 Sarah Carrick's resignation was announced and she left in November after almost five years; she was replaced by Amanda West, who was welcomed to her first meeting in September 2007, when Peter Todd was appointed as Assistant Manager. Amanda had succeeded Joan Cave as Deputy Manager and in 2008 Sonia Weston, the current manager, was appointed on a job-share basis with Samantha Powell; Sonia became Manager in September 2015 when Amanda West left.[23] Sally Rogers, the current Deputy Manager, was promoted to that post in September 2019.

Adult Education 100
This was an important report on adult education, coming 100 years after the 1919 report; its origins were described thus:

Early in 2018 a group of adult educators, recognising the historic importance of the 1919 Ministry of Reconstruction Adult Education Committee's final report, set up the Adult Education 100 campaign. It wished to encourage a programme of activities, centred on the centenary of the 1919 report, which would both recover and re-evaluate the twentieth-century history of adult education, and set out a vision for life-wide adult education for the century ahead.[24]

The campaign had four themes: the 'Centenary Commission', composed rather like the Ministry of Reconstruction Adult Education Committee, and with essentially the same brief; research and educational projects concerning the history and record of adult education, ranging from adult education classes and undergraduate student projects to research funded by research councils; archival and curatorial projects to preserve the records of adult education; and 'knowledge exchange' activities to build public discussion about the role and significance of adult education. Several well-known public figures took part, as well as academics; it was chaired by Dame Helen Ghosh, Master of Balliol College Oxford. It made eighteen recommendations based on six key focuses: framing and delivering a national ambition; ensuring basic skills; fostering community, democracy and dialogue; promoting creativity, innovation and informal learning; securing individual learning and wellbeing; and attending to the world of work. Focus no. 4 (promoting creativity, innovation and informal learning) is seen as particularly pertinent to the Settlement, although elements of all six have relevance. In its conclusion the report said:

> Lifelong learning needs to be about individual benefit and fulfilment as well as productivity at work and social engagement – although the enhanced mental and physical health that is associated with education will in turn benefit the economy and society. A far greater investment in lifelong learning will pay off in every sense. There is no benefit to be had from further delay.

Other matters

In 1980 John Armitage, the co-owner of David's Bookshop, left money for an annual lecture in his name.[25] The *Encyclopaedia Britannica*, for which Armitage worked, gave £200 towards the lecture programme. Shirley Williams gave the first lecture on 23 January 1981; her title was 'Making people matter',[26] and the lecture was a sell-out. In 1984 it was hoped that the Armitage Memorial Lecture would continue for another five years and in fact they continued for another ten years (there is a full list of speakers at the end of this chapter). The last lecture was in 1994 when it was becoming increasingly difficult to find suitable speakers. The bank account was transferred to the Settlement on the understanding that a programme of occasional lectures would be arranged and the remaining money was put into a newly named Lecture Fund. In 1986 Michael Wood, the television presenter and historian, gave a one-off lecture about the BBC Domesday project, which was another sell-out.[27]

Many local groups used the Settlement for their meetings and continue to do so. They included the Marriage Guidance Council, Gingerbread, Nomads cycling club, table tennis, ballet and Friends of the Disabled. A big increase in new members was reported in September 2009.

In 1985 Mr Hawke from North Herts College spoke on 'The Aims and Directions of The Settlement', which he said was 'the oldest community centre in Letchworth'.[28] The following year John Cruse gave a summary of his thirty-seven years' association with the Settlement; he was presented with an engraved goblet and an etching of the building, as well as a cheque. In July 1986 the Women's Adult School, which had met at the Settlement for many years, closed; it had been in existence for eighty years.[29]

In September 2000 Miss Williams accepted the nomination as president and expressed her honour at following Mr Cruse. As part of the centenary celebrations of the world's first garden city in 2003, it was agreed to produce a wall-hanging and Dr Schofield's design was accepted. The wall-hanging now takes pride of place in the Kincaid Hall (see plate 9).

In November 2000 there was an application to the Arts Council of North Herts for £640 for a keyboard, overhead projector and the cost of removing the old piano. There were plans to celebrate the centenary of the Skittles Inn in 2007, with a members' dinner and entertainment in March, and an exhibition in May. In July a new mission statement was agreed: 'The Letchworth Settlement exists to provide a social centre for education and recreation, open to all, in a friendly, accessible and supportive atmosphere.' In September 2007 Joan Williams stood down as president and was succeeded by John Hall and he, in turn, was succeeded in 2014 by John Bird, who had been treasurer for ten years. In 2016 Rosalind Whitehouse, a conservator, restored the portrait of the first warden, James Dudley, by the Rev A J Bamford.[30] The cost of this was met by Roy Evans as a tribute from the last warden to the first.

The Settlement's second half-century was one of enormous changes, but it weathered the many storms and emerged stronger. The founders of the Settlement would have been amazed at the changes over the last 100 years but enormously satisfied that their 'baby' had grown and matured. One thing they could not have predicted was the global pandemic, Covid-19, which in early 2020 led to a lockdown in the UK and other countries. All venues in the UK were closed, including the Settlement, but a number of Settlement tutors delivered distance-learning courses for those students able to access them. The hope was that this would keep the spirit of the Settlement alive until the building could be re-opened, and classes and other activities could resume.

List of John Armitage lecturers

1981	Shirley Williams	1988	Jonathon Porritt[37]
1982	Jo Grimond[31]	1989	Bryan Magee[38]
1983	Gerald Priestland[32]	1990	Nicholas Friend[39]
1984	Dr Norman Moore[33]	1991	Rabbi Julia Neuberger[40]
1985	John Maynard Smith[34]	1992	Prof David Marquand[41]
1986	Baroness Warnock[35]	1993	No lecture that year.
1987	Very Rev Michael Mayne, Dean of Westminster[36]	1994	Terry Waite[42]

26   Terry Waite with Joan Williams, on the occasion of his Armitage lecture in 1994.

Endnotes

1 See chapter 6 for details of what was taught.
2 See chapter 7 for more information.
3 Now the Letchworth Centre for Healthy Living (<https://www.letchworthcentre.org/about-us/our-history/>). It began life as a children's isolation hospital, serving Letchworth and Hitchin, and was briefly a children's convalescent home. See <https://www.nationalarchives.gov.uk/hospitalrecords/details.asp?id=420> for information from the Hospital Records Database.
4 This was owned by Bedfordshire County Council and had been a teacher training college.
5 Information from Pam Burn.
6 It is not clear if this was the same Tabor who was treasurer in 1922 but it is unlikely.
7 Annual report, 1973/74; <https://en.wikipedia.org/wiki/Three-Day_Week>.
8 Natural gas was discovered off the coast of Britain in 1965 and from 1967 to 1977 all properties were converted from town gas to natural gas.
9 Annual report, 1983/84.
10 Garden City Collection, LS 7/T.
11 Annual report, 1984/85.
12 Information from the current chairman, Pam Burn.
13 Garden City Collection, 2018.21.40.31C.
14 <http://settlement-players.co.uk/history/supplement/>.
15 Information from Roy Evans.
16 Information from Sarah Carrick, former manager.
17 See <https://fcccommunitiesfoundation.org.uk/> for further details.
18 <https://api.parliament.uk/historic-hansard/lords/1973/may/23/adult-education-the-russell-report>; <https://thelearningage.wordpress.com/2013/04/20/what-was-margaret-thatchers-legacy-to-adult-education/>.
19 For details on courses, see chapter 6.
20 <https://api.parliament.uk/historic-hansard/commons/1991/may/20/education-and-training>.
21 Minutes still held at the Settlement.
22 Ditto, for November 2000 to October 2007.
23 Interviews with Sarah Carrick and Sonia Weston.
24 See <https://www.centenarycommission.org/>.
25 He was the London editor of the *Encyclopaedia Britannica* from 1949 to 1965.
26 She was the MP for Hitchin from 1964; see <https://en.wikipedia.org/wiki/Shirley_Williams>.
27 This was a national project carried out between 1984 and 1986 to celebrate the 900th anniversary of Domesday book. Its aim was to create a modern version of William the Conqueror's famous survey of the wealth and resources of his kingdom. Throughout the UK, school children and other researchers collected huge amounts of information about the communities in which they lived. This information, in the form of text and photographs, was recorded onto two 12-inch videodiscs that could be viewed using a BBC master computer connected to a special videodisc LV-ROM player. Further details can be found on the National Archives' website.
28 At the 1985 AGM.
29 The men's adult school had closed much earlier; see LS 7G, meeting on 7 December 1935.
30 Information from Pam Burn. Alfred John Bamford painted it in 1927 and he died two years later; North Hertfordshire Museum holds some of his paintings.
31 See <https://liberalhistory.org.uk/history/grimond-jo-lord-grimond/>.
32 See <https://en.wikipedia.org/wiki/Gerald_Priestland>.
33 See <https://en.wikipedia.org/wiki/Norman_W._Moore>.

34   See his obituary, <https://www.theguardian.com/news/2004/apr/22/guardianobituaries. highereducation>.

35   See <https://en.wikipedia.org/wiki/Mary_Warnock,_Baroness_Warnock>.

36   See <https://www.westminster-abbey.org/abbey-commemorations/commemorations/michael-mayne>; he was vicar of Norton from 1965 to 1972.

37   Garden City Collection, LS 7U.

38   See <https://en.wikipedia.org/wiki/Bryan_Magee>.

39   See <https://inscapetours.co.uk/about/>.

40   See <https://en.wikipedia.org/wiki/Julia_Neuberger>.

41   See <http://davidmarquand.co.uk/>.

42   See <https://aru.ac.uk/graduation-and-alumni/honorary-award-holders2/terry-waite>.

Chapter 6
WHAT WAS TAUGHT?

I t is interesting to compare what was taught at the Settlement over the last 100 years and how this has changed over time. Much would have been dictated by changing needs and fashions, but the student base also altered over this period. The earliest syllabus for which there is a record is for the autumn term 1920, which would have been the very first one.[1] Four tutors are listed: Mr W H Corbett, Miss M Ibberson, Miss A D F Salmond, MA and James Dudley, MSc (the warden). The syllabus quotes from *Settlements and their Work*:

> A Settlement is a group of men and women associated under qualified leadership for the common pursuit of knowledge, wisdom, and fellowship, and for the service of the community, either by personal effort, by united action, or by influencing public opinion and participating in public life.

There were four 'special' opening lectures, 'free and open to all'. Basil Yeaxlee, BA, the Joint Secretary of the Educational Settlements Association, gave the first one on Monday, 20 September, on 'Education through Settlements'. This was followed the next day by G D H Cole, the author of *Self-Government in Industry*, *Social Theory* and other books, on 'Economic Studies in Adult Education'. Wednesday saw Henry Wilson, the president of the Arts and Crafts Exhibition Society, talk on 'Industry or Education' and the final speaker was Major J T Bavin, of the YMCA music section, who talked about 'Education in Music' on the Friday.

Starting in late September or early October, there was one class each weekday. On Mondays the warden lectured on 'Geology (General and Local)'; Miss Ibberson's course, held at 16 Common View, was 'Appreciation of Music'; the warden lectured again on Wednesdays, this time on 'Economics'. Thursday's course was on 'Industrial History', given by Mr Corbett ('of Hitchin') and Friday saw Miss Salmond lecture on 'English Literature'. In addition, there was a

What a Settlement is.

A SETTLEMENT is a group of men and women associated under qualified leadership for the common pursuit of knowledge, wisdom, and fellowship, and for the service of the community, either by personal effort, by united action, or by influencing public opinion and participating in public life.

From "Settlements and their Work."

SPECIAL OPENING LECTURES

Monday, Sept. 20th, 1920, at 7.45 p.m.

BASIL A. YEAXLEE, B.A.
(Joint Secretary, Educational Settlements Association)

"Education through Settlements"

Tuesday, Sept. 21st, at 7.45 p.m.

G. D. H. COLE
(Author of "Self-Government in Industry," "Social Theory," etc.)

"Economic Studies in Adult Education"

Wednesday, Sept. 22nd, at 7.45 p.m.

HENRY WILSON
(President, Arts and Crafts Exhibition Society)

"Industry or Education"

Friday, Sept. 24th, at 7.45 p.m.

MAJOR J. T. BAVIN
(of the Y.M.C.A. Music Section)

"Education in Music"

These opening Lectures are free and open to all.
COLLECTION.

Letchworth Adult Educational Settlement

Museum Buildings, Town Square,
LETCHWORTH.

Syllabus
for the
Autumn Term

Sept. 20 to Dec. 17, 1920

Tutors :

Mr. W. H. CORBETT
(W.E.A. Class)

Miss M. IBBERSON
(Diplomée, Dresden Conservatorium)

Miss A. D. F. SALMOND, M.A.
(Gold Medallist in English)

JAMES DUDLEY, M.Sc.
(Warden)

Garw Press, Letchworth.

SATURDAY, December 11th

Members' Social and Conference

PEARSALL TRUST.

Class in "History"

Rev. F. A. HIBBERT, M.A.
(Late Headmaster of Denstone College)

DETAILS LATER.

CLASSES:

MONDAYS *at* 7.45 *p.m.*
(Starting September 27th)

"Geology (General and Local)"

J. DUDLEY, M.Sc.

In connection with this course practical work and excursions will be arranged.

TUESDAYS *at* 7.45 *p.m.*
(Starting October 5th)

"Appreciation of Music"

(WITH MUSICAL ILLUSTRATIONS)

MISS M. IBBERSON
(*Diplomée, Dresden Conservatorium*)

This Class will be held at No. 16, Common View.

WEDNESDAYS *at* 7.45 *p.m.*
(Starting September 29th)

"Economics"

J. DUDLEY, M.Sc.

THURSDAYS *at* 7.45 *p.m.*
(Starting September 30th)

Workers' Educational Association Class in

"Industrial History"

W. H. CORBETT (of Hitchin)

FEE - 2/6.

Secretary - Mi.. MOR, 71, Norton Road

FRIDAYS *at* 7.45 *p.m.*
(Starting October 1st)

"English Literature"

Period to be discussed with the Class

Miss A. D. F. SALMOND, M.A.

A Teachers' Club

meets on Mondays from 5 to 7.30 p.m.

Hon. Secretary - - Miss D. MAY

The Warden expects to hold Classes at ARLESEY on Tuesday evenings and at BALDOCK, Thursdays.

FEES:

Each Subject: 5/- for full course of about 22 Lectures (September to March), or 2/6 per term.

Payable at the opening lecture of the course or term.

Fee includes use of Reading Room, open every week day from 12 noon to 9.30 p.m.

Classes in Chemistry, Woodwork, Public Speaking and Conversational French

are also contemplated and will be arranged if 12 or more members enrol.

The Warden will be glad to consider suggestions for other cla..

27 & 28   Earliest syllabus, autumn 1920. GCC 2018.21.1.51

teachers' club on Mondays evenings, whilst the warden expected to hold classes at Arlesey on Tuesday evenings and at Baldock on Thursdays. Fees were 5s for a full course of about twenty-two lectures, or 2s 6d for a single term. Classes in chemistry, woodwork, public speaking and conversational French were also contemplated and would be arranged if twelve or more members enrolled. In addition, the Pearsall Trust had arranged a class in history, to be given by Rev F A Hibbert, MA, headmaster of Denstone College between 1905 and 1919.

The syllabus for the summer term 1921 showed quite a few changes.[2] Tuesday's class was now a 'League of Nations Union Study Circle', given by the warden, a Regional Survey course was given by a number of different lecturers on Wednesdays, and on Thursdays there was a 'Reading and Dramatic Circle' (which was formed during a 'Literary and Social Evening' held at the Quaker meeting house, Howgills). The Naturalists' Society organised a series of nature-study rambles on Tuesday evenings, from 26 April, plus a number of special events. As well as a lecture on 'Industrial Art' by Douglas Cockerell and one on the Keats centenary by Prof A A Cock, folk dancers visited Barley WI and a members' and students' tea, social and conference were held, also at Howgills. Courses proposed for the autumn term were economics, American history, European history, geology, public speaking, appreciation of music and chemistry. The choice of subjects to teach would have been dictated by what it was felt students would benefit from and the availability of tutors.

By autumn 1921 some, but not all, of the proposed classes were running; in addition, there were others on the history of the growth of government and

Letchworth Adult Educational Settlement

LECTURE by RT. HON.

VISCOUNT HALDANE

" RELATIVITY AND EINSTEIN "

In the PIXMORE HALL,

SATURDAY, NOVEMBER 12th, 6.30 P.M.

UNRESERVED SEAT   6d.

29   Ticket for Haldane lecture, 1921. GCC LBM4074.15.55

conversational French. Miss Ibberson gave three courses on music appreciation, two of them on the same evening!

Because accommodation was limited in the museum, other venues were used, such as the Girls' Club, Boys' Club and Howgills, as well as some local schools. Beginning in the autumn term 1921 there was also a series of Saturday chamber concerts. The spring 1922 syllabus lists meetings of the Students' Fellowship and the Executive Committee, as well as a book sale.[3] The syllabus for the 1922 summer term included a class on woodwork for Girl Guides and an art class taken by Alec Hunter[4] 'with open-air sketching when weather permits'. The warden lectured on five modern novelists – H G Wells, Samuel Butler, Joseph Conrad, Arnold Bennett and John Galsworthy.[5]

A report in *The Citizen* on 24 April 1925 referred to reviving university extension lectures, but only two years later the same newspaper reported that the warden thought they had been proved unsuitable for the Settlement's needs and should be discontinued.[6] In January 1926 it was stated that it had not been possible to continue the Russian lectures.[7] This refers to a series on 'Russian life and literature', first given in October 1925 by Mr Konstantin Nabokov, late Russian Chargé d'Affaires in London and uncle of the author Vladimir Nabokov.[8]

The syllabus for the spring term 1927 included a three-year tutorial class on psychology.[9] Ten years later, it was so successful that the same tutor, Mr Daisley, was to give one on philosophy.[10] The *Beds and Herts Pictorial* of 2 October 1928 discussed the possibility of developing a parish history of Letchworth along the lines of Reginald Hine's work on Hitchin; Mr Hine gave practical advice in his lecture and it was proposed that a group of researchers be formed.[11] *The Citizen*, later the same month, gave advance notice of a course in biology; it would explain the nature of the subject and its usefulness in combating lethal diseases such as cancer and leprosy:

> Hitherto clever and stupid, strong-willed and weak-willed men and women have come into the world in a haphazard fashion and the evolutionary process seems to have been a matter of chance or luck. With the advance of biology it may be possible to assist in the creation of men and women whose mental, moral and physical make-up far surpasses anything we know now. The course was to be to be taught by Mrs Mary Adams over three winters.[12]

In November 1928 the warden reported that a history group was now engaged in local research.[13] The well-known economic historian, Eileen Power, gave a lecture on 'Life and Letters in Fifteenth Century England' on 26 April 1929, in association with the Pearsall Trust.[14] A series of lectures on town planning and citizenship was suggested in June 1929, with the idea that the Settlement should be the centre for the study of the ideals of the founder of the garden city movement, Ebenezer Howard; it is unclear if they took place.[15]

By the end of the first decade, the number of language classes had increased; in the summer term of 1929 elementary and advanced Italian was offered, as well as elementary and intermediate French. Miss Ibberson was teaching a choral class at Meppershall, and an instrumental one at Weston. Rev F Thatcher, MA, gave a course of three or four lectures on 'The problem of unemployment' and Miss C Cockerell offered a course of six lessons on embroidery.[16] The summer fair, held on 15 June, was opened by the Hitchin historian Reginald Hine and featured plays, puppets, music and an outdoor pageant.

Lists of classes start to appear in the annual reports. That for 1929–30 reported the increasing development of vocational classes such as printing, electricity and magnetism, which were thought to attract younger people. Mr Cockerell gave two lectures on the history of printing illustrated from his own valuable collection of books. The reports also give the average attendances at classes and in 1929–30 the most popular course was at Graveley, on local history, with an average attendance of sixty. This was exceptional, as the next nearest were two courses which each attracted an average of twenty-four.[17] A typed list of classes from 1930–31, which includes brief details of the students' occupations, shows that economics had fifty-one in the class, followed by elementary German with thirty-four and elementary French with thirty. Those working in factories, shops or offices made up sixty-five per cent of the students, eleven per cent were teachers, seven per cent were 'leisured' and sixteen per cent had 'home duties'.[18] The syllabus for the spring term 1933 included free classes for the unemployed, during a period of great economic depression.[19]

A report in the *Advertiser* on 25 September 1930 said: 'The meeting on October 14th will be addressed by Mr E M Forster, the well-known author of *A Passage to India*, and other novels. It may be of local interest to say that Mr Forster has lived at Stevenage and the scene of his novel *Howard's End* is laid in this part of the county.'[20] *The Citizen* reported on the talk in its 17 October issue: 'Mr Forster said the book was tied up with the age in which it was written – in fact the novel was the mirror of its age. In it could be found the political and religious thought of the day, as well as tricks of speech and attitude to life.'[21]

A scheme to bring in Cambridge University extra-mural classes was reported in November 1930.[22] A list of classes from 1931 to 1932 makes interesting reading; they included special lectures on Henry Ford, string games of primitive peoples, the evolution of French art and weather forecasting, the last by Mr S Wilkinson, head of the grammar school. There were two debates, on tariff reform vs free trade and 'Is socialism a cure for our present ills?', as well as wireless discussion groups, on 'Should Britain starve?' and 'The disintegration of the modern world order'.[23] The following year there were lectures on 'The aims of life and the use of leisure' (by Sir Arnold Wilson, MP), 'Letchworth village and its history' (Reginald Hine), 'Medieval dovecotes' (Mrs Lumley Ellis) and 'Rock climbing' (Mr W Lewin).[24]

THE CITIZEN, NOVEMBER 9th, 1934.

Mr. C. H. Chaplin, of Baldock, at the Settlement on Tuesday. See report below.

30   Mr Chaplin demonstrating the use of a lathe, November 1934. GCC 2018.21.11.42

A summer school for teachers on bookbinding was held from 20 to 31 July 1931: 'The Council of the Letchworth Adult Educational Settlement have arranged for a short training course in Bookbinding to be held in the Settlement building under the direction of Mr Douglas Cockerell, teacher of Bookbinding at the LCC Central School of Arts and Crafts and Lecturer to the School of Librarianship, University College London.'[25]

The *Advertiser* of 12 October 1933 reported on a talk about James Joyce to the Literary Circle; it was given by Mr Claud Sykes, who was described as a personal friend of Joyce, their friendship of sixteen years' standing having begun in Switzerland during the war. Joyce and his wife had visited Letchworth in 1929.[26] Another prestigious speaker was Miss Bowie, who was due to speak on 26 January 1934: 'The Literary Circle of the Settlement is looking forward to the visit of the secretary of the English Verse-Speaking Society, Miss Bowie, who will speak on Verse and give illustrative readings... The Verse-Speaking Society has as one of its supporters Mr John Masefield, the Poet Laureate. It is a compliment to Letchworth's well-known Literary tastes that the secretary herself is coming.'[27] In February 1934 'Miss Elizabeth Jenkins, Letchworth's youngest novelist, lectured to the Settlement Literary Circle on Friday last, when her subject was Oliver Goldsmith.'[28]

Local history continued to be popular. In 1934 a summer project was a field club to study natural and local history, the members of which would undertake the making of lantern slides to illustrate their discoveries.[29] The local history group had obtained access to documents relating to Letchworth Manor; they had made several expeditions and had spent a considerable amount of time 'deciphering old documents', the results of which Mr Hine had used in recent lectures.[30] Another local history class, run on informal lines by Mr C Flemming, 'aroused much interest' and was followed up by expeditions to various places of interest in the neighbourhood.[31]

National and international issues were also covered; *The Citizen*, on 2 February 1934, said: 'Fascism may invade England says German visitor. An eloquent warning that the powers of Fascism might invade England at any moment was made by Dr Lothar Frey, speaking on "Fascism as an Expression of the European Crisis" at the Settlement on Tuesday.'[32] The following year it said: 'An interesting discussion on the question of the peace of the world will be opened on Friday, February 1st, at the Settlement by the Rev Dugald Macfadyen.'[33] There was a joint weekend lecture school on Germany in the post-war world on 6 and 7 April 1935, which consisted of three lectures by Harold F Bing, MA, and brought together the adult schools and the Settlement.[34]

A JOINT WEEK END LECTURE SCHOOL

Arranged by the Three Adult Schools and the Adult Education Settlement.

ON APRIL 6 th, and 7 th, 1935.

A Course of Three Lectures by HAROLD F. BING, M.A.

on

GERMANY IN THE POST WAR WORLD.

I — SATURDAY 3. 15. p.m.
Post War Germany and the Rise of Nazism.

SATURDAY 6. 30. p.m.
2 — The German Youth Movement and its influence in other Countries.

SUNDAY 3. p.m.
3 — Foreign Policies in Post War Europe and the effect on them of the Rise of Nazism.

Full Course Ticket : One Shilling   Teas provided each day
Single Lecture : Sixpence   at Ninepence each.
          Ample time allowed for Questions and Discussion.

31   Weekend conference on Germany, 1935. GCC 2018.21.16.7

BOARD OF EDUCATION GRANT-EARNING CLASSES, 1939-40

Class	No. Enrolled	Students who have completed two-thirds total attendances
Three-year Course (Cambridge Extra Mural)		
Philosophy (H. H. Daisley, M.A.)	18 ...	11
One Year		
Music Appreciation (Sidney Twemlow, B.Mus.)	20 ...	4
Terminal		
Autumn Term. Literature—Makers of the English Essay (The Warden)	19 ...	17
Spring Term. Literature—John Milton (The Warden)	10 ...	7
Short Terminals		
Spring Term. Literature—Enjoyment of Poetry (The Warden)	19 ...	12
Summer Term. Literature—Diaries and Journals (The Warden)	14 ...	11
Autumn Term NON GRANT-EARNING		
Health Exercises (Miss Childe-Warren) ...	14 ...	12
Folk Dancing (Miss Felix)	31 ...	20
Embroidery Group	9 ...	6
Italian (Miss Borissow)—Elementary ...	7 ...	6
—Advanced	4 ...	3
Local History Group (Mr. Flemming) ...	7 ...	5
English for Foreigners (The Warden and Mr. Picton-Sommers)—Elementary	8 ...	4
—Advanced	20 ...	7
—Grammar	19 ...	7
Spanish Group (Mr. A. Scrutton, A.I.L.) ...	4 ...	2
Settlement Orchestra (Mr. Owen) — Later merged in L.E.A. orchestra	10 ...	8
Spring Term (Tutors as in Autumn Term)		
Health Exercises	8 ...	7
Folk Dancing	22 ...	10
Embroidery Group	7 ...	5
Italian—Elementary	7 ...	5
—Advanced	5 ...	5
English for Foreigners—Elementary	6 ...	5
—Advanced	8 ...	3
Summer Term (Tutors as in Autumn Term)		
Health Exercises	8	
Folk Dancing	18	
Italian—Elementary	7	
—Advanced	4	**Village Classes**
German Conversation	8	
French Advanced	12	**Holwell, 8 & 14**
Tailoring (L.E.A.)	16	
Orchestra (L.E.A.)	19	

L.E.A. CLASSES, 1939-40

One Year Courses

Subject	Students 1939	1940	Percentage attendance of members during complete course
Tailoring (Miss Gallard)	17 ...	14 ...	82.1
Tailoring (Miss Gallard)	20 ...	18 ...	79.7
Tailoring—Senior (Miss Gallard) ...	18 ...	17 ...	70.8
French—Elementary (Miss Wallace, B.A.)	30 ...	25 ...	59.0
—Advanced (Miss Borissow) ...	18 ...	31 ...	51.4
Orchestra (Mr. Youngman, A.C.P.) ...	16 ...	19 ...	72.3

32   1939/40 annual report, list of classes.

Visit of distinguished South American mountaineer

TIBOR SEKELJ, F.R.G.S.

will speak in Esperanto (with English translation) on
" TWICE ON THE SUMMIT OF ACONCAGUA "
at
The Settlement, Nevells Road, Letchworth
on SATURDAY, SEPTEMBER 3, at 7.30 p.m.
SHORT FILM   ALL WELCOME
1/6, including refreshments Arranged by the Esperanto Group.
ax

33 Notice of Sekelj lecture, 1949. It was given in Esperanto with an English translation. GCC LBM4074.15.230

FENCING AT THE SETTLEMENT

One of the latest ventures at the Letchworth Settlement is the fencing class. Instruction is given by expert fencers and the ladies as well as the men are taking a keen interest. This photograph by Patrick Jago shows pupils in action.

34 New fencing class, 1956. GCC LBM4074.15.279

The *Advertiser* of 11 April 1935 carried a report: 'Mr Harold Bing of Hull University spoke on European policy since the war and its responsibility for the Nazi regime in Germany. He described the state of despair produced in every class of society and the consequent welcome given to Hitler, whose programme might make things better and could not make them worse.'[35]

In December 1935 the Men's Adult School decided to discontinue their meetings and offered their surplus funds of 14s 9d to the Settlement; it is unclear why it felt unable to continue.[36] A curious talk was reported in *The Citizen* on 3 July 1936, given by Mr Picton-Sommer, on 'Sunbathing'. One of his suggestions was 'if technically possible, the two flat roofs on the Letchworth Swimming Pool should, by surrounding them with low screens, be made available for sun worshippers, so that real sunbaths could be taken there, on the one terrace for men, on the other for women'.[37] Naturism was very popular in the 1930s, so it is hardly surprising that Letchworth would wish to participate in it.

The 1936/37 annual report said that a class in pewter work had been formed at the request of the adult school and that the most successful County Council classes were tailoring, leatherwork and Esperanto.[38] An Esperanto Club was formed but by 1956 it was reported to be in difficulties, presumably in attracting enough members.[39] Nevertheless a lecture was given by a 'distinguished South American mountaineer' in Esperanto.

During the second world war, the Settlement tried to run as many classes as it could. On 26 July 1939, just before the outbreak of war, it was said that LEA classes would continue except for drawing and German; the warden hoped that the Council would reconsider the latter.[40] A report on the Letchworth Evening Institute for the 1939–40 session stated that German classes were very popular.[41] In the summer term 1939 two English classes for foreign students were being held each week, mainly as a contribution to the refugee problem, and were well attended.[42] *The Citizen* reported on 20 September 1940: '…despite unsettled times the Letchworth Settlement has reopened this week with an unusually full and interesting syllabus'. Classes included tailoring, health, the evolution of the piano and Elizabethan virginals. Dr Marion Cockerell[43] gave instructions in child welfare and hygiene, as described in chapter 3; Mrs Cobb took a sewing and craft class to enable students to make children's clothes and Christmas gifts, and the warden and his wife held a weekly afternoon social for evacuees.[44]

The warden received a letter from the British Drama League on 28 March 1958. The Settlement had asked it to provide some lectures on drama; an earlier attempt had clearly not been a success:

The first one was in 1951 and was a practical course which seems to have been much appreciated but poorly attended. At that time Mr Davies was the warden. Then, in 1952, Mr Groombridge was warden and we were asked to run a rather more academic type of course on Twentieth-Century Theatre. There was quite a lot of correspondence over the programme for this course because the Educational Centres Association were insistent that the Course should be of an academic nature and the lecturers we chose were all highly qualified graduates of Oxford or Cambridge. All the lecturers felt at the end of this course that it had been the wrong type of course for the people attending because they had no particular interest in the theatre and no background of knowledge and again attendance was very poor. One lecturer said that there seemed to be a few elderly people who had just come in to keep warm and also some small girls of about 12 years old.[45]

The 1959/60 annual report said that two of the most successful classes were 'An approach to art' and 'Some modern novels'; they were held in the afternoon with audiences almost entirely of women, adding that there seemed to be little interest in one-time popular political and economic subjects.[46] A letter from the University of Cambridge Extra-Mural Board on 13 July 1961 confirmed arrangements for a class to be held on 'Race Relations' by Mr R E Pahl, BA. It described the content: 'Colour in Britain. This section will consider the background of the migration of coloured people to this country and the social problems that ensue. Local examples will be taken where possible and the implications of policies to control immigration discussed.'[47] It is clear that the Settlement was not shirking difficult subjects and it would be enlightening to know whether the course was seen as successful.

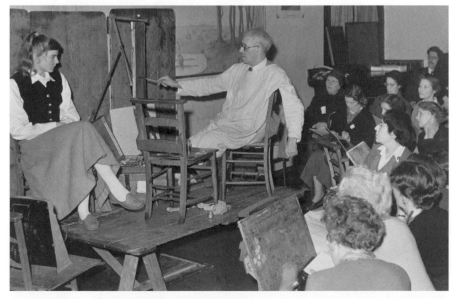

35　Art class, nd. Arts and crafts have always featured a lot in Settlement classes. Like so many photographs in the archives, we have no further details about this one. Neither the tutor nor the model has been identified.

Another letter from the Board on 24 July 1961 referred to a class called 'Social and Economic Relationships in Industrial Societies', to be taught by Mrs L Lockwood, MA.[48] The content included trade unions, the welfare state and social stratification.[49]

By the early 1960s, there were more afternoon classes.[50] Ten years later, there were more morning classes and more craft courses; the Settlement was now open on three mornings, four afternoons and five evenings a week, plus some weekend activities.[51] This was a gradual change from the earliest days, when the courses only ran in the evenings, to accommodate students who were working full-time. The student base had changed and now included more retired people and those who did not need to work full-time. Three pre-retirement courses were held as a result, in conjunction with local firms, and by the end of the 1960s there was a programme of short courses.[52] One titled 'Beauty Forum' aroused so much interest that three courses were arranged and a fourth planned for those on the waiting list.[53] Unfortunately, there is no information about what was covered in the course. In a sign of the times, a course called 'Decimal Currency for the Housewife' was held in February 1971.[54]

36   Fashion show, 20 May 1971. GCC FGCHM588.283

COURSE SUMMARY: 1988/89

*	Aspects of 20th Century Music	Mr D.B. Fielder	U	20	A,S.	13	480
*	18th Century English Art	Mrs I. Woodward	U	20	A, S,	36	1086
*	British Landscape (3rd year tutorial)	Mrs G. Sheail & Dr R.E. Randall	U	24	A, S, u	27	1130
*	Elizabethan & Stuart England	Mr G.A. Curry	U	10	A	42	708
*	America: 1st 300 Years	Mr G.A. Curry	U	10	S, Su	34	574
	Conservation of Historic Towns & Villages	Dr M. Miller	U	10	A	13	204
	Weather, Climate, Society	Mr A.H.C. Carter	U	20	A, S	10	354
	Churches, Stained Glass & Furnishings	Mr R.K. Hagen	U	20	A, S, Su	18	606
*	Upholstery 102	Mrs B. Boardman	NHC	20	A, S	16	602½
*	Upholstery 103	Mrs B. Boardman	NHC	20	A, S	20	705
	Upholstery 104	Mrs B. Boardman	NHC	20	A, S	20	855
*	Upholstery 205	Mrs B. Boardman	NHC	20	A, S	20	507½
*	Dressmaking 105	Mrs B.J. Raines	NHC	20	A, S	17	554
*	Creative Stitchery	Mrs V.E. Aitken	NHC	20	A, S	15	444
*	Art	Mrs V. Lewis	NHC	20	A, S	15	482
*	Yoga 101	Mrs P.A. Hancock	NHC	20	A, S	18	373½
*	Yoga 202	Mrs P.A. Hancock	NHC	20	A, S	13	279
*	Yoga 303	Mrs P.A. Hancock	NHC	20	A, S	22	484½
	Yoga 404	Mrs S. Hamilton	NHC	20	A, S	16	396
	Yoga 406	Mrs S. Hamilton	NHC	20	A, S	20	508½
*	Keep Fit 207	Mrs C.B. Evison	NHC	20	A, S	28	389
*	Keep Fit 208	Mrs C.B. Evison	NHC	20	A, S	24	362
*	Calligraphy 311	Mrs J. Cooper	NHC	10	A	16	256
*	Calligraphy 403	Mrs J. Cooper	NHC	10	S	13	192
*	Melodrama to Modern Drama	Mrs J. Bransby	NHC	10	A	11	147
	Patchwork & Quilting	Mrs M. Pallett	NHC	10	A, S	18	242
*	Yoga 1011	Mrs P.A. Hancock	NHC	10	S, Su	14	184½
*	Yoga 2021	Mrs P.A. Hancock	NHC	10	S, Su	16	171
*	Art e 3021	Mrs V. Lewis	NHC	8	S, Su	12	148
*	Creative Stitchery 2011	Mrs V.E. Aitken	NHC	6	S, Su	17	180
*	**Melodrama to Modern Drama**	**Mrs J. Bransby**	**NHC**	**10**	**S**	**13**	**168**
*	**Calligraphy 304**	**Mrs J. Cooper**	**NHC**	**10**	**S**	**17**	**270**
*	Calligraphy 401	Mrs J. Cooper	NHC	10	S	19	328
*	Keep Fit 2071	Mrs C.B. Evison	NHC	12	S, Su	25	233
*	Keep Fit 2081	Mrs C.B. Evison	NHC	12	S, Su	20	198
*	Upholstery 106	Mrs B. Boardman	NHC	12	Su	29	517½
*	Yoga 3031	Mrs P.A. Hancock	NHC	10	S, Su	20	229½
	Yoga 4051	Mrs S. Hamilton	NHC	10	S, Su	22	279
	Yoga 4061	Mrs S. Hamilton	NHC	10	S, Su	19	250½
	Upholstery 1041	Mrs B. Boardman	NHC	6	S, Su	13	140
*	Upholstery 1021	Mrs B. Boardman	NHC	6	S, Su	13	162½
*	Upholstery 1031	Mrs B. Boardman	NHC	6	S, Su	13	147½
*	Upholstery 2051	Mrs B. Boardman	NHC	6	S, Su	10	140
	Patchwork & Quilting	Mrs M. Pallett	NHC	5	S. Su	10	76

KEY TO ABBREVIATIONS:- A = course held during the daytime.

S.H. Student Hours

U = Course sponsored by University of Cambridge Board of Extra-Mural Studies

NHC= Courses sponsored by North Herts College

IN ADDITION regular meetings of many groups and organizations were held, as well as piano and flute lessons, and ballet lessons.

37 1988/89 annual report, list of classes.

Yoga became the latest course to attract many students; courses were first held in the early 1970s and by the early 1980s five separate classes were running.[55] New courses were added all the time and by the 1990s it was reported that maximum use was being made of the building.[56] In 2004 it was estimated that between 42,000 and 50,000 people used it each year.[57] The shift away from evening classes continued, so that by 1990 most were held during the day.[58] Cambridge University courses continued and these were generally held in the evenings; in 2003 it was stated that the Settlement was the biggest provider of them in the area.[59] It was reported that the Certificate in English local history (a two-year course) was very demanding[60] and in 2006 that potential students were put off the university courses because of the need to do course work.[61] Very shortly afterwards, because the government cut funding for non-academic courses and it would have made them prohibitively expensive, there were no more Cambridge University Extra-Mural courses; some of the tutors were re-employed and paid by the Settlement on a different footing.[62] In January 2009 it was reported that most of the tutors were willing to work with the Settlement.[63]

Over the past six years the Settlement has undergone more changes, in an effort to attract new and younger members whilst also retaining its loyal core. Shorter courses and weekend workshops have become very much part of the programme and new and different courses have been introduced, from encaustic wax painting to learning to use an iPad or tablet. It is possible to plot the changes through the annual brochures which show what was taught and give details of the tutors. In 2020 classes and short courses can be grouped into a number of subject areas such as arts and crafts, languages and fitness, but there is a long list of special-interest ones which cannot be easily classified. A few examples will suffice: Lip-reading; 'Great advances in physics'; 'Oxygen, the breath of life'; criminal psychology; and 'Remembering the Beatles'.

Endnotes

1   Garden City Collection, 2018.21.1.51.

2   Garden City Collection, 2018.21.1.13.

3   Garden City Collection, 2018.21.1.33.

4   See chapter 2 for more on Hunter.

5   Garden City Collection, 2018. 21.1.42.

6   Ibid., 2018.LS 7C, meeting on 11 June 1927.

7   Ibid., 2018.21.44.56.

8   Ibid., 2018.21.5.11(a).

9   Ibid., 2018.21.8.2.

10 1936/37 annual report.

11 Ibid., 2018.21.10.2.

12 Ibid., 21.10.9, 21.10.12; LS1 J, 19 October 1928. It is unclear who Mrs Adams was.

13 Ibid., LS 7D.

14 Ibid., LS 7C.

15 Ibid., LS 7D.

16 Ibid., 2108.21.10.66.

17 1929/30 annual report.

18 Garden City Collection, LS 7F.

19 Ibid., 2018.21.16.26.

20 Ibid., 2018.21.13.9.

21 Ibid., 2018.21.13.14.

22 Ibid., LS 7D.

23 1931/32 annual report. The building of a wireless set is dealt with in chapter 4 .

24 1932/33 annual report.

25 Garden City Collection, 2018.21.23.11 & 12.

26 Ibid., 2018.21.15.181.

27 Ibid., 2018.21.15.133.

28 Ibid., 2018.21.15.146.

29 Ibid., LS 7G.

30 Ibid., LS 7I.

31 1936/37 annual report.

32 Ibid., 2018.21.15.139.

33 Ibid., 2018.21.16.22; see also <https://en.wikipedia.org/wiki/Dugald_Macfadyen>.

34 See <https://menwhosaidno.org/men/men_files/b/bing_harold.html>.

35 Garden City Collection, 2018.21.16.55.

36 Ibid., LS 7I.

37 Ibid., 2018.21.17.155.

38 1936/37 annual report.

39 Garden City Collection, LS 7Q.

40 Ibid., LS 7O.

41 Ibid., 2018.21.23.96. The Letchworth Evening Institute was run by the County Council and put on mainly vocational classes, including some at the Settlement.

42 Garden City Collection, 2018.21.23.81.

43 Douglas Cockerell taught at the Settlement and this was his second wife, they married in 1914; see <https://www.oxforddnb.com/view/10.1093/ref:odnb/9780198614128.001.0001/odnb-9780198614128-e-32474?rskey=UUo1aR&result=6>.

44 1939/40 annual report.

45 Garden City Collection, 2018.21.25.25.3.

46   1959/60 annual report.
47   Garden City Collection, 2018.21.25.3.
48   Ibid., 2018.21.25.4.
49   Ibid., 2018.21.25.4.
50   See, for example, the 1961/62 annual report that refers to three afternoon classes.
51   1970/71 annual report.
52   1967/68 annual report.
53   1968/69 annual report.
54   Garden City Collection, LS 11B.
55   Annual reports for 1970/71, 1971/72, 1981/82 and 1988/89.
56   1991/92 annual report.
57   Minutes of a meeting on 12 November 2004.
58   1989/90 annual report.
59   Minutes of meeting held on 7 November 2003, still held at the Settlement.
60   1994/95 annual report.
61   Minutes of meeting held on 25 September 2006, still held at the Settlement.
62   Information from Sarah Carrick. The first reference in the minutes is from 12 November 2007.
63   Minutes of meeting held on 5 January 2009, still held at the Settlement.

Chapter 7
KEY FIGURES

O ver the 100-year life of the Settlement, there have been many people whose involvement has been crucial, but inevitably many more who will remain unsung. This chapter looks at the wardens of the establishment, as well as briefly mentioning other key figures.

The wardens
The Golden Jubilee in 1970 was marked by a brochure which listed all the wardens up to that date. The complete list of wardens is:

James Dudley, MSc	1920–28
Herbert Ernest Milliken, BA	1928–30
Ruth Isabel Pym	1931–38
John Short	1938–41
H. Mary Richards, BA	1941–48
Cedric Percival Davies, BA	1948–51
Brian K Groombridge, MA	1951–55
John Waller, BA	1955–58
J G Hughes, LLB	1959
J Malcolm Page, BA	1959–63
Roy A Evans, BA	1963–2001

As described in chapter 5, the job title changed to 'Administrator' in 1992 and to 'Manager' in the year 2000, the title still used today. At the Management Committee meeting on 12 September 1978, John Armitage presented a beautifully printed list of the wardens going back to 1920, and it was agreed to have it framed and hung in the building.[1]

James Dudley, MSc, 1920–28

Dudley was a key figure in the Settlement movement. After his death at Cartmel, Cumbria on 18 March 1950, the journal of the Educational Settlements Association, *The Common Room*, carried an appreciation of him. It began by saying he was:

> …one of that rare company of men and women who, in the last fifty years, believed in the 'Evangel of Adult Education', and who carried their belief to the point of leaving all, turning their backs on security, burning their boats, that they might be more wholly committed to so great a cause; men and women who avoided, rather than sought, a prominent place in the front line of publicity; men and women who were gifted, disciplined scholars with broad human sympathies and the faith and the courage of pioneers.[2]

He was born in Sheffield in 1876 and educated at Bradford Technical College, and Leeds and London universities. At first he worked as a mathematics and science teacher, but from 1920 devoted himself wholly to adult education. After the end of the first world war, the Ministry of Reconstruction set up a committee on adult education, which published an important report in 1919. It referred specifically to educational settlements; this idea apparently caught the imagination of a group of people in Letchworth, and in their initial discussion of the idea in May 1920 they invited Dudley to meet them. It is unclear how the founders of the Settlement knew Dudley, but he may have been familiar to them through work he was doing in this field.

As a result, they asked him to establish an educational settlement in Letchworth, to provide for people resident in the 'Garden Suburb' [*sic*] and to extend adult education to the local villages.

The article in *The Common Room* went on to describe Dudley's work at Letchworth, although it doesn't mention him specifically:

> At the outset, in September 1920, the Settlement had no 'home', no programme and no students, but in the course of the first month one hundred men and women were enrolled for classes which were accommodated in three rooms at the Museum. In the course of the next seven years a suitable property was secured and the Educational Settlement had a home of its own; the number of weekly classes and lectures rose from 8 to 29, and enrolments from 120 to 610… Contact was made and maintained with twelve of the surrounding villages, and members of the groups and classes in those villages paid visits to the Educational Settlement, and groups of players and musicians visited the Villages… The Educational Settlement in Letchworth, now under a young and enterprising Warden [Cedric Davies], is to-day an outstanding example, in the county, of what a centre for adult education should be.[3]

The article goes on to praise Dudley:

> James Dudley brought to this new undertaking a surprising versatility; he was by education and training a mathematician and scientist, and by disposition he was an artist; he was conversant with the great literatures of the world and could lecture authoritatively on scientific, literary and historical subjects; he was a sensitive and discriminating art critic and he had an unusual knowledge of music in addition to being a musician of considerable talent.[4]

Dudley was one of the founders of what became the Educational Settlements Association, and chairman of its Executive Committee from 1933 to 1946. In 1927, shortly after he was invited to go to Germany by the World Association of Adult Education, he was invited to become the Principal of 'Avoncroft Residential College for Rural Workers', which he accepted. This was set up by George Cadbury and others, to provide agricultural education for farm labourers and was based in Bromsgrove, Worcestershire; Dudley had been asked for his advice and help in setting it up.

He remained in post at Avoncroft until 1940. In a further tribute the article said:

> James Dudley possessed the qualities which enabled him to evoke the confidence of men, even the most shy and retiring, and also to inspire them to grapple with and grasp knowledge that would enable them to to be more competent and useful men. His personal interest in men may be judged by the fact that during each long vacation he endeavoured to visit every student who had been accepted for the coming year, and thus to establish friendly contact with them in their own county, their own village and their own home.[5]

When Avoncroft college closed in 1940, because of the war, Dudley and his wife Agnes moved to Cambridge. The article concludes: 'In counsel he was wise; in friendship he was faithful; and his life, like that of other true educationists, was part of that "creative interaction of religion and culture" which eludes the historian but which is the power that makes history.'[6]

Dudley's salary was discussed at the Council meeting on 10 June 1925, as it was considered inadequate for all the work he did; £325 was considered to cover the administrative and pioneer work, but it was felt that he should be paid extra for taking classes.[7] At a special Council meeting on 27 July 1927, his appointment at Avoncroft was reported but that his acceptance was on condition that he could stay at Letchworth for another year. His leaving party was fixed for 30 April[8] and it was reported in *The Citizen* on 11 May 1928; £600 had been raised and a bound book with the names of all those who had

38   Portrait of Rev Alfred John Bamford, nd. GCC LBM1186

taken part in fund-raising inscribed.[9] At the Council meeting on 9 May 1928, it was stated that Mr Cockerell was making a gift of the whole presentation book, including the cost of the writing, and that the Educational Settlements Association had appointed Dudley as its representative on the Council, so that Letchworth would still benefit from his advice and knowledge. As described in chapter 5, A J Bamford had painted a portrait of Dudley; he would either present it himself or sell it to anyone who would present it, giving the purchase money to the Fund;[10] the portrait was recently conserved (see Plate 2). Barry Parker, Mr Bamford and Dr Yeaxlee spoke of the fine work done by Mr Dudley during his eight years at the Settlement and of their great regret at his departure.[11] The annual report for 1927–28 also referred to Dudley's departure, saying: 'One tangible asset has remained at the Settlement – a life-like portrait of Mr Dudley, painted by Mr Bamford.'

Herbert Ernest Milliken, BA, 1928–30

Milliken (whose forenames were never recorded in the official records of the Settlement) came to the Settlement from Malvern College where he had been an Assistant Master.[12] He was born in Allestree, Derbyshire in 1889 and died on 28 October 1955, in Essex.

The Common Room of June 1928 carried an update from the Letchworth Settlement: 'The change of Wardenship of our Settlement is probably well-known, with its mixed feeling of sadness in bidding goodbye to Mr James Dudley and of joy in welcoming our new warden Mr H E Milliken.'[13] The *Beds and Herts Pictorial* reported on the students' fair in 1928 at which Mr Benjamin Cherry, a Chancery lawyer, spoke highly of Milliken.[14]

At the Council meeting on 24 March 1930, it was reported that the warden had been asked by the World Association for Adult Education to take a bursary for the purpose of studying adult education in Austria for two or three months, to report on educational progress in Vienna and the country districts there. His visit took place in the summer term of 1930.[15] Very soon afterwards, Milliken tendered his resignation as he had been appointed to a post in the adult education department of the BBC.[16] In *The Citizen* of 21 November 1930 he said that 'he was not going because he was tired or bored with the work, but because he could see he was too expensive for them'.[17] At the meeting of the Executive Committee on 23 January 1932 it was reported that a framed enlargement of Mr Milliken had been offered by anonymous donors and accepted.[18]

Ruth Isabel Pym, 1931–38

The Citizen of 3 July 1931 reported on the students' annual fair. Mrs Pryor of Lannock Manor opened it and spoke about the warden, Miss Pym:

Letchworth Settlement was very lucky in its warden, Miss Pym, for the speaker did not think they could have anyone better, because as well as having the right sort of ideas, she attended to the details, which was very necessary in running such an institution. Miss Pym also had wonderful pulling power, enabling her to do things and also making other people do things which otherwise they would not do…[19]

The annual report of 1937/38 referred to her resignation, along with one of the tutors:

We have had two great shocks during the year, firstly in the departure of Miss Thompson, who did such effective work both as teacher of Art and Crafts and also in the office; Miss Pym had reigned over us for seven years, and it is to her wise rule and devoted labours that the Settlement owes its continued success. Her enthusiasm knew no limit, no difficulty dismayed her, no peril daunted her; she made the most unlikely people into willing helpers and knew how to get the most out of the rustiest machine![20]

The following year it was reported that Miss Pym had returned as the 'organiser of the collectors', but it is unclear what this role entailed.[21]

The Citizen of 16 August 1946 referred to Miss Pym's death; it was reported in more than one newspaper and there were several articles about her. Her address was given as Meadow Way Green, Letchworth, but she died at Alciston, Sussex. She had come to Letchworth in 1910 and was involved with the co-operative housing scheme at Meadow Way Green. She was a suffrage campaigner, mainly in Surrey before the first world war. She served in France during the war and became involved with the League of Nations. In Letchworth she helped Mary Ibberson to found the Hertfordshire Rural Music School. She did a lot of work in the villages: 'In spite of her age – she was 73 – after a hard day's work she would climb into what has been described as "her ancient car" and drive off to some remote village, in the cold and darkness, along dangerous roads.' Barry Parker added a glowing tribute:

We speak of people as 'Letchworth Pioneers' merely because they came to Letchworth in its early days… If Ruth Pym undertook anything, everyone knew it would be conscientiously, thoroughly and completely carried through… A pioneer in the best sense, she came to Letchworth in the true pioneering spirit, believing in Garden Cities and to take her part in establishing the first.[22]

Two years after her death a memorial was created, somewhat surprisingly taking the form of a tea trolley; at a meeting on 22 March 1948 the inscription was agreed: 'In appreciation of the work of Miss Ruth I Pym, Warden 1931–

39   Newspaper photograph of John Short, 1941, from *The Citizen*.

1938'.[23] The 1950/51 annual report said that a 'handsome portrait' of her had been commissioned and presented to the Settlement by Mr Falk, the chairman.[24]

John Short, 1938–41

The 1937/38 annual report, while lamenting Miss Pym's resignation, said: '…we have great hopes that our new Warden, Mr John Short, will in his own way bring new life and efficiency to our cause'. An interesting survival is a handwritten report of the Selection Sub-Committee meeting, held on 4 July 1938.[25] The committee had met four times and some of these meetings had lasted for over two hours. The post had been advertised in *The Times* and *The Friend*, and enquiries made at Fircroft College (Birmingham), Cambridge University and privately. There had been thirty applications, eight of whom were women, and private enquiries were made about ten of the applicants. Three candidates were interviewed but no final decision was made. After a week's consideration and further private enquiries, the committee met again and unanimously agreed to recommend Short, at a salary of £250 a year; he was to start on 1 September 1938 and would be non-resident.

Short was born in November 1911 in Lancashire and educated at Kelsick grammar school, Ambleside, Fircroft College, Bournville, and Balliol College Oxford. He apparently left school early 'owing to family difficulties', served his time as an apprentice landscape gardener, worked for a year with the Church Army, was awarded a bursary to Fircroft and from there gained an Extra-mural

Scholarship to Oxford, where he had spent the previous three years. He had passed the qualifying examination for the degree of BLitt, and was writing his thesis in order to graduate. He was president of the university English club, editor of *Cherwell*, and a member of the university Dramatic Society; he was very interested in music and had written verse and reviews for *The Listener*, *Time & Tide* and other publications. Short was quoted as saying:

> My interest in Adult Education is genuine because I have gained from it more than I can hope to estimate… It seems to me essential that one should constantly try to think of the adult student in terms of his milieu – his work, family anxieties and responsibilities. This does not mean that I believe in either spoon feeding or a cheap popularisation of what is worth while in life, which is only too common nowadays; I have gained most from a disciplined course of reading. But it does seem to me that one has to seek to understand people as individuals and to try to give to each person the materials for his own development and the encouragement and help he needs. On the other hand, whilst my interests are primarily in country life and in the preservation of that sort of life, I do think that one has to try to put facilities for hearing good music and enjoying contemporary drama and poetry within the reach of people living in provincial or rural areas.[26]

Among material still at the Settlement is a brief biographical note about Short, written by Angela Beese in December 2008; she says that it was based on her ongoing research, including interviews and correspondence with his daughter, members of his former wife's family and the 'archivist at Letchworth Educational Settlement'.[27] Much of what she wrote is covered by the report above, but she added that his maternal grandfather was a Lakeland shepherd who loved reading and who would always take a book with him when working on the fells. Short married Edna Cureton in Birmingham in June 1939.

The *Advertiser* reported on his appointment on 14 July 1938: '[Mr Short] recognises his own debt to Adult Education, and is eager to do all he can to further the movement and to help others as he himself has been helped.'[28] In a message to the students on 8 September, Short said that he was as proud of their new table tennis set and recreational facilities as he was of the syllabus.[29]

At first, the outbreak of the second world war had little effect and Short clearly went above and beyond for his students, as reported in the 1939/40 annual report: 'The Warden throughout this time managed to keep together his Drama class at Holwell; walking to the class when transport facilities were unobtainable, and on one occasion at least cut off by snow drifts and obliged to spend the night in a farmer's kitchen!' He did work for the Citizens Advice Bureau, Social Service Committee and Letchworth Youth Committee. He served on the Welfare Committee of the Ascot Government Training Centre and delivered three lectures to Indian students on English life and customs; he also gave a series of lectures to the troops on current affairs, under the auspices of the Army Education Corps.[30]

Nevertheless, he was liable to be conscripted, and at the Executive Committee meeting on 8 November 1940 it was reported that he had been before the Hardship Committee and had received exemption until the following February; this might be extended up to three times.[31] The following April it was stated that the only grounds on which he could appeal was the time necessary to complete his thesis. The Executive Committee recommended that Mrs Short be appointed co-warden with her husband and that, if he was called up, she should be paid a salary representing the difference between the service or government pay of Mr Short and his previous salary as warden.[32] On 12 May 1941 a special meeting was called to discuss Short's probable call-up. Mrs Short declined the offer, principally because a six-month probationary period was required. Barry Parker wrote to Ernest Bevin:[33]

...on the grounds that Mr Short would be of greater value to the Country in his position as Warden of the Settlement having regard to the fact that it was of first class National importance that the 50 Indian Students (and more to follow) at present being trained at the Letchworth Government Training Centre should be provided with adequate and carefully planned social activities, and lectures on English life and customs, such as Mr Short could on behalf of the Settlement provide. The fact that there was insidious defeatist propaganda going on in Letchworth was to be stressed and an interview sought between Mr Barry Parker, Mr Hazelton and Mr Bevin.[34] Any further arrangements should be deferred until this had been settled.

Mrs Short was again assured of the Council's fullest confidence and support, should she take over her husband's duties, but she declined on the main grounds that she felt the wardenship was really a man's job 'in these difficult times'. It was decided to advertise for a temporary warden in the *Times Educational Supplement*, *The Friend* and the *New Statesman*; to specify a man, ineligible for active service and only during the absence of the present warden. Nineteen applications were received whilst nine others had not applied after being sent the particulars. By the meeting on 23 July 1941, four more applications had been received; one was to be followed up and the particulars of a previous applicant were to be investigated. After further discussions, only a Mr Nottridge was invited for interview. He was a conscientious objector but exempted from military service on medical grounds; he apparently gave satisfactory replies to the questions.

A meeting of the Council was held on 29 July 1941 to decide questions of policy: (1) was a man with comparatively poor qualifications to be engaged or a woman with good qualifications; (2) if the latter, was the post to be advertised?

Miss Pym and the secretary were asked to arrange to see a Miss Richards, so as to be in a position to give any required information about her. It was also agreed that Short's salary was to be paid until the end of August. By now, there were 24 applications; two had outstanding qualifications but were ineligible because they were conscientious objectors,[35] and the rest of the men were not up to standard. There had been three applications from women and it was decided to consider them without re-advertising. It was eventually agreed to appoint Miss H Mary Richards, BA, subject to the approval of the Executive Committee and ratification by the Educational Settlements Association.[36]

At the AGM on 15 November 1941 it was reported that Short had gained his BLitt. The following AGM, on 14 November 1942, received messages of goodwill from him; he had been promoted to the Army Education Corps. At the Executive Committee meeting on 8 June 1945 the question of Short's return was discussed, and it was unanimously decided to ask him what his plans were; there was no possibility of an increase in salary. In the meantime, Miss Richards was asked to continue with arrangements for the syllabus for the following year.[37] At the next meeting of the committee, on 23 July 1945, a letter from Short was tabled, in which he stated his definite desire to return to the Settlement and asked whether the committee intended to apply for his release under Class B.[38] It was unanimously decided that there were no grounds for applying for his release earlier than his ordinary demobilisation number. He was to let the Council know immediately he had definite news of his demobilisation, as Miss Richards must have time to make the necessary arrangements. Her salary was to be secured until 31 August 1946 and she agreed to give the necessary notice if she obtained a new post in the interim. It was reported on 26 September 1945 that Short was to have a testimonial as the only means of getting an earlier release; this had been written by 30 October and Short asked that reference be made to the duties of a warden besides his teaching. The Council, at its meeting on 19 December 1945, agreed to use the County Council grant to increase the warden's salary by £150, bringing it up to £400.[39]

According to the notes by Angela Beese, Short was horrified to be passed as fit for military service, and his experience of war left him deeply traumatised, which affected his mind for almost the rest of his life. She said that he had lost his job and 'accepted a teaching post in Folkestone which was beyond his capabilities, causing him additional stress.' It is unclear how accurate this was; a letter written by Short to the Executive Committee was entered in the minutes of 17 July 1946:[40]

> I am given to understand that the present Warden is anxious to remain in office, and I do, of course, appreciate the desire for continuity in view of the protracted course of the War, which has kept me away so long on Active Service. I had always looked forward to

coming back to the Settlement (as stated in my correspondence on the subject of Class "B" release) and I had been disappointed that I had not received the courtesy of an Annual Report, and some account of the development of the Settlement whilst I was serving. However, I hope that I may hear more regularly in future, for the welfare of the Settlement will always be my keenest interest.

In view of the apparent difficulties of re-instatement at the Settlement, I have now decided to take advantage of an opportunity to take up my academic interest again, and my many friends at the Settlement will be pleased to know that I hope to complete some new research which has been well received by the authorities to whom I submitted it.

It was decided to organise a collection for Short and to recommend to the Council that Miss Richards become the permanent warden. Short trained at the Emergency Training College in Folkestone between 1947 and 1950. A collection of his poems, *The Oak and the Ash*, was published in 1947 by J M Dent, who were based in Letchworth.[41] Angela Beese said that his mental health deteriorated, as did his marriage, and in 1950 he left Edna and their young daughter and returned to Ambleside. He apparently became a familiar figure walking the roads in the area and took a job washing dishes in a local hotel. He died in Folkestone in 1991. According to Angela Beese, after he died his estranged daughter, who was his next-of-kin, received a demand from the library for a book which he had borrowed and which had not been returned; it was his own book. The poet Vernon Scannell gave a broadcast on BBC Radio 4 on 22 September 1993, entitled 'The Long Search for Mr Short', about his search for the talented but elusive poet John Short, whom he eventually ran to earth in strange circumstances; tantalisingly, the synopsis from the *Radio Times* does not give any more details.[42]

Mary Richards, BA, 1941–48

Mary Richards' degree, from Cardiff, was in English, German and economics. She had helped to organise a branch of the WEA in Hertford, where she lived before coming to Letchworth.[43] The 1940/41 annual report said: 'Miss Richards brings to her new post an infectious enthusiasm and a genuine love of hard work and has already become very popular with the Students.' Miss Richards' resignation in 1948 is dealt with in chapter 3.

Cedric Percival Davies, BA, 1948–51

Davies' appointment was reported at the Council meeting on 21 July 1948 and he was welcomed to the AGM of the Students' Fellowship shortly afterwards.[44] Two newspapers, *The Citizen* of 27 August 1948 and the *Herts Pictorial* of 1 September 1948, reported on his appointment. The former said that he was married with three children and that:

40 Sketch of Mary Richards by Margaret Townsend, 1942.

The Council were impressed equally by his outstanding academic qualifications and his very wide experience in industry. Before proceeding to the university he was engaged for nine years in the cotton industry as an operative in various departments, including weaving, and eventually on the administrative side.[45] His daily contact with workers, clerks and management personnel will prove invaluable in his new post. It will be of interest to many readers to know that although Mr Davies has not hitherto lived in Hertfordshire, his mother's family has resided in the county for over 300 years.[46]

Davies attended Sidcot Friends' school in Somerset, was given an unconditional exemption from war service as a conscientious objector and took up the teaching of 'backward' children before going to Manchester University, where he gained a degree in English Literature and Language.[47] He succeeded to his father's title on 29 December 1950 as Lord Darwen; the title had only been created for his father in 1946.[48] At the Council meeting on 25 May 1951, it was reported that he had accepted another job: 'a new position in London, which was better paid, with more responsibility and more interesting to Davies, as head of the training and education department of the National Association of Mental Health'.[49] What sounds like a lively leaving party from the Settlement was reported in the local press.

Brian K Groombridge, MA, 1951–55
Brian Groombridge's appointment was reported at the Council meeting on 7 September 1951. He was twenty-five and had served for three years in the RAF. His Cambridge MA was a tripos in moral sciences and history. He had had various jobs, including as a WEA tutor and lecturer. He had not been interviewed at first, because he was comparatively young, but the Selection Committee was confident that his qualifications, academic and personal, would more than outweigh this apparent drawback.[50] His appointment featured in *The Citizen* on 7 September 1951:

Twenty-five years old Mr Brian K Groombridge, bright, genial and friendly, whose young head rests on experienced shoulders… is the new warden at the Settlement. He took an early liking for the Garden City; he likes the people he has met so far, he thinks he will like many others… To get an insight into real life he took many jobs during vacations…

There are no further references to him until his resignation was reported at the Management Committee meeting on 22 March 1955.[51] There was a tribute to him in the 1954/55 annual report; he was going to the settlement in Rugby.[52]

41 Newspaper photograph of Malcolm Page, 1963, from *The Citizen*. GCC LBM4074.15.320

John Waller, BA, 1955–58

There is practically nothing known about Waller beyond the dates of his tenure. His appointment was recorded at the Council meeting on 2 June 1955 and he was to start on 1 September following.[53] In October 1958 it was reported that he was taking up a new post the following January as a tutor at Linton Village College, on a starting salary of £550 a year.[54]

J G Hughes, LLB, 1959

The sole reference to Hughes is at the Council meeting on 2 June 1959, when he offered to resign a month early, in view of his recent absence through ill health, which was agreed.[55]

J Malcolm Page, BA, 1959–63

Similarly, there is practically nothing about Page, about from a couple of articles in the local press.[56] One referred to his engagement and subsequent marriage: he married Angela MacLennan at All Saints' church, Chelsea, on 21 December 1961. The couple received a cheque from the Settlement as a wedding present.[57]

At the Management Committee meeting on 24 January 1963 it was reported that he was on the NJC scale for youth leaders, starting at £700 a year. He felt it was time to seek a new position, but no explanation was forthcoming. He offered his resignation from 31 August.[58]

Roy Evans, BA, 1963–2001
Evans' appointment was confirmed on 12 June 1963 at a starting salary of £940 a year; he would live in the Settlement flat at a rent of £2 a week. *The Citizen* of 17 September 1965 included an article by him, entitled 'The Settlement passes another milestone'. There is a photograph of him and the caption says that he was thirty and keenly interested in all problems concerning adult education, adding: 'He takes a special interest in local history as well as international affairs. Before coming to Letchworth he taught history at a Bedfordshire grammar school.'[59] At the Management Committee meeting on 22 April 1971 Roy was congratulated on being elevated to the bench.[60] At the 1980 AGM the president, Mr Spinks, said that he had known all the wardens, but that Mr Evans worked twice as hard as any of them.[61]

Other staff
Mary Ibberson, Sub-Warden and music teacher, 1920–29
Apart from the wardens, undoubtedly the most important person connected with the Settlement in its early days was Mary Ibberson, who went on to found the Hertfordshire Rural Music School. At the Executive Committee meeting on 22 September 1922 she was appointed as the warden's full-time assistant and the Educational Settlements Association agreed to pay her salary.[62] The title of 'Sub-Warden' was created in 1923 and she was acting warden for a time in 1926, as described in chapter 3.

Much of what we know about her life and career can be found in her book, *For joy that we are here. Rural Music Schools 1929–1950*, published in 1977. After studying music abroad for four years, she returned to England in 1913 and to Letchworth, as she describes:

…to Hertfordshire and the early, idealistic days of Letchworth, which as the First Garden City, had a bewildering number of activities very attractive to a young woman in her twenties. Folk dancing, for instance, which was a revelation to me; the women's suffrage movement which gave me some practice in public speaking; and above all Girl Guides…

As tutor-in-training [the title of her first post] I was given the task of giving short courses in music appreciation, a subject made popular by the enthusiastic work of Dr Percy Scholes and Sir Walford Davies…[63]

The book gives considerable detail about how she taught music, including in the villages, and how she established the Rural Music School. The fact that it still exists, as Benslow Music, is a tribute to her hard work and enthusiasm, and her incomparable contacts.

42   Mary Ibberson, from the preface to her book.

43   Ken and Gwen Spinks cutting a cake at their golden wedding anniversary, 1976.

There are occasional references to other employees. One interesting document that has survived relates to the role of caretakers, when Mr and Mrs Higgs were appointed in 1936.[64] They were to serve in various related capacities for twenty-seven years and their retirement was reported at the 1963 AGM.[65] The document outlines their duties, and includes the application form that Tom Watson Higgs filled in. He was forty-two, married and with one daughter, aged eleven. He gave Mr Waugh of the Country Gentleman's Association as his referee, as he was at that time employed there; this was in a lower position than formerly and he was finding it difficult to make ends meet.

Letchworth Settlement has been fortunate in the calibre of officers who have worked for it, in some cases for many years and in different roles. Many have already been mentioned, but there are countless others whose hard work and enthusiasm have greatly contributed to its longevity and success.

Endnotes

1 This has sadly not been found.
2 *The Common Room*, summer 1950, pp. 14–15.
3 Ibid.
4 Ibid.
5 Ibid.
6 Ibid.
7 Garden City Collection, LS 7D.
8 Ibid., Council meeting on 4 April 1928.
9 Ibid., 2018.21.9.39.
10 This refers to the £600 that was raised; it appears to have been used to pay off the outstanding debt on the building.
11 Council meeting on 4 April 1928.
12 1927/28 annual report, held at the Settlement; Garden City Collection, GCC 2018.21.4.35. I am grateful to Philippa Parker for the biographical information.
13 *The Common Room*, June 1928.
14 Garden City Collection, 21.10.3/4.
15 1929/30 annual report.
16 Garden City Collection, LS 7D, Council meeting of 4 October 1930.
17 Ibid., 2018.21.13.25.
18 Ibid., LS 7G. The portrait does not seem to have survived.
19 Ibid., 2018.21.13.64.
20 1937/38 annual report.
21 1938/39 annual report.
22 Garden City Collection, LS 5A; 2018.21.51.194.
23 Ibid., LS 7O; the trolley is currently located on the stage in the hall and is used by the Settlement Players (see colour plate 5).
24 This can be found in the Green Room adjacent to the hall.
25 Garden City Collection, LS 7O.
26 Ibid.
27 Presumed to be Roy Evans.
28 Garden City Collection, 2018.21.18.96.
29 Ibid., 2018.21.23.95.
30 1940/41 annual report.
31 Garden City Collection, LS 7O.
32 Ibid.
33 Minister of Labour in the wartime government; see <http://www.bbc.co.uk/history/historic_figures/bevin_ernest.shtml>.
34 Garden City Collection, LS 7O.
35 It is not clear why this barred men from applying but many employers took a similar attitude; see <https://spartacus-educational.com/2WWco.htm>. Nottridge, referred to above, was not ruled out because he was exempt from military service on medical grounds.
36 Garden City Collection, LS 7O.
37 Ibid.
38 See <https://en.wikipedia.org/wiki/Demobilisation_of_the_British_Armed_Forces_after_the_Second_World_War>.
39 Garden City Collection, LS 7O.

40   Ibid.
41   See <https://en.wikipedia.org/wiki/J._M._Dent>.
42   See <https://genome.ch.bbc.co.uk/ad82282854f3422a8506e24656461479>.
43   Garden City Collection, education box 3.
44   Ibid., LS 7P.
45   In his father's factory.
46   Garden City Collection, LS 5C, 2018.21.53.53.
47   Annual report, 1950/51.
48   See <https://en.wikipedia.org/wiki/Baron_Darwen>; his father was the only Quaker peer at the time.
49   Garden City Collection, LS 5E, 2018.21.55.
50   Ibid., LS 7S.
51   Ibid.
52   Ibid., LS 5G, 2018.21.57; *Herts Pictorial*, 1 April 1955.
53   Ibid.
54   Ibid.
55   Ibid.
56   Ibid., education box 3.
57   *The Pictorial*, 10 November 1961; *The Citizen*, 29 December 1961.
58   Ibid., LS 7S.
59   The photograph was taken by Donald Brunt, who was heavily involved with the Settlement.
60   Garden City Collection, LS 7T.
61   Ibid.
62   Garden City Collection, LS 7A.
63   *For joy that we are here. Rural Music Schools 1929–1950*, p. 5.
64   Ibid., 2018.21.16.10.3.
65   Ibid., LS 7S.

Chapter 8

LOCAL GROUPS AND ORGANISATIONS

From the very early days of the Settlement, there have been clubs connected with it. Their members are usually students at the Settlement, and all have to pay the membership fee. Today they pay to hire a room based on the numbers in the club and the frequency of their meetings. Other organisations hire rooms on a fixed rental, such as the Letchworth Arts & Leisure Group. Over the century, many groups have come and gone but there are some that have a long history of involvement with the Settlement. The more important ones are dealt with in this chapter but inevitably others will have left little trace of their existence.

The Settlement Players

The Players' history is nearly as long as that of the Settlement itself, being formed in 1923. We are fortunate that there are two accounts, one covering the first forty years and the other the following decade. Sadly, there is nothing from 1983 onwards, although records survive for anyone wishing to research its history. The first account was written by Inga Horwood,[1] who has since moved away from the town but who has generously agreed to allow her work to be used. The second one was written by the late Noel Ripley[2] and his grandson has given permission for his work to be included. The records in the Garden City Collection, principally the newspaper cuttings, give copious coverage of the Players, and it has only been possible to scratch the surface in this chapter.

The first production was *The Little Plays of St Francis*, three one-act plays by Laurence Housman, and the first night was on Wednesday, 19 December 1923 at Ashwell village hall. Two more performances were given in the Co-operative Hall in Letchworth and at the then Three Counties Asylum in Arlesey. Inga Horwood's history gives copious details of every production, including the cast and production staff; anyone interested is encouraged to look at it online. There are some amusing anecdotes and reminiscences which bear repeating. Evan John Simpson, the first producer, kept a notebook which 'is full of candid little comments about his cast'. He listed the group's assets at the end of their first six months, including a sedan chair, seven tea chests, two orange boxes, battens and canvas, a cube-sugar box and various other oddments. Apparently, these items could be transformed to look like part of a wall with ornamental gate, newell post and iron railings. Simpson left notes for his successor, including that Rev Gerrard Kerr Olivier, father of Sir Laurence and rector of St Mary's Letchworth, would supply a cassock if required.

In January 1927 it was reported that there was a prospect of the revival of the Players, which suggests that it had folded, but this is not mentioned in Inga Horwood's history. Many Letchworth people enjoyed the theatre, both professional and amateur, and repertory companies frequently performed in the town. One called the Ben Greet Players[3] featured a young Laurence Olivier in its production of *Macbeth*, put on at the theatre belonging to St Christopher School, now St Francis' College, which had been opened by Ellen Terry.[4]

There were other amateur dramatic groups, such as the Letchworth Dramatic Society;[5] in 1937 SPADS (St Paul's Amateur Dramatic Society) was formed and still flourishes today.[6]

In 1925 the Players moved to the Skittles Inn, where they used the former bowling alley as their theatre. James Dudley started a course of drama reading classes and members of the Players travelled to some of the villages to teach dramatic techniques; one of those involved was Ken Spinks, who was to be involved with the Settlement Players for most of his life.

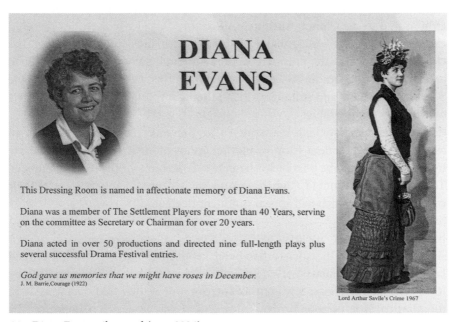

DIANA EVANS

This Dressing Room is named in affectionate memory of Diana Evans.

Diana was a member of The Settlement Players for more than 40 Years, serving on the committee as Secretary or Chairman for over 20 years.

Diana acted in over 50 productions and directed nine full-length plays plus several successful Drama Festival entries.

God gave us memories that we might have roses in December.
J. M. Barrie, Courage (1922)

Lord Arthur Savile's Crime 1967

44   Diana Evans tribute, nd (post 2004).

In 1929 the Mimes Group met for the first time and was surprisingly popular, continuing until 1955. The new stage was a great fillip and in 1956 the warden, John Waller, took a part in *The Alchemist*. Diana Stead, who married Roy Evans, joined the cast in 1963; in September that year the Players joined forces with SPADS to present *1903 – And So What?*, with a script written by Hugh Bidwell and Donald Griggs.[7] To quote Inga Horwood's account, 'Throughout the history of the Players it has been the unstinted and dedicated work of a comparatively small number of people which has left its stamp on the Society and contributed so much to the theatrical life of the Garden City.'

Noel Ripley's Supplement, covering the years 1973 to 1982, continued the practice of naming all the productions, with their cast, crew and press coverage. It is to be hoped that someone will produce another history, covering the years since his account. In March 2008, following a request from the Settlement Players, it was agreed to name two dressing rooms 'Evans' and 'Elson' after Diana Evans and John Elson, both of them long-standing supporters of the Settlement and of the Players. The most recent production, in March 2020, was *Queen Margaret*.[8]

Letchworth Garden City Camera Club

Robert Staddon has kindly supplied some information on the history of the club. It was formed on 13 October 1921 following the demise of the K & L (Kryn & Lahy) Photographic & Microscopic Society.[9] Its meetings were held in Letchworth Museum but when it was told that smoking was not allowed, the club moved to the Church Institute on Pixmore Way. Early meetings involved the development of plates, making lantern slides and gaslight printing. The club moved back to the museum in 1924 although some meetings were held at Donald Brunt's studio in Leys Avenue and other venues. It moved to the Settlement in 1950 and still meets there; the Brunt Room always has a display of members' photographs.

The Settlement student magazine, *The Eye and the Trumpet*, noted in May 1928: 'The Camera Club is another innovation. If sufficient people are interested, it should be possible to arrange a dark room for the use of members. The Letchworth Camera Club have also invited our members to join their rambles, a list of which will appear on the notice board.'[10]

Settlement Music Society

A minute book of the society has been kept, covering the decade between January 1951 and January 1961; it is presumed to have been compiled by Joan Williams. There are few items of interest, but at the AGM on 4 May 1953 the warden, Brian Groombridge, said: '...[he] was very much impressed by its work. There was a spirit of adventure about the concerts and we were not

45   Kryn & Lahy Camera Club, nd (pre 1921). GCC LBM70.206

46   Camera Club exhibition opening, 12 March 1954. GCC LBM3056.14.62

47   Camera Club outing to Finchingfield, nd.

merely a group coming together to have a good sing or play but met with a serious purpose.' Joan Williams succeeded Mr Groombridge as chair of the Music Society at the AGM on 2 May 1955. The orchestra was disbanded in July 1960[11] and this was reported in the 1964/65 annual report; it is not clear what happened in the intervening period.

In October 1922 the musical appreciation class turned itself into the Settlement Music Lovers' Club; it had a new venture, the formation of a class for elementary orchestral practice.[12]

Campers Club

In 1922 the warden hoped that this club would be able to have a standing camp near Letchworth during the summer months.[13] That year *The Citizen* said: 'As a result of a successful week-end camp held at Weston at the end of the summer, the Student Fellowship of the Adult Education Settlement have formed a campers' club. They plan weekends in the summer and a holiday camp of a week or 10 days by the sea.'[14] A second camp was held in May 1923 in a field by Lannock Manor, owned by Colonel and Mrs Pryor.[15]

In June 1927 the number of members was increasing under Kenneth Spinks' leadership and in July 1928 two very successful camps were held at Biggleswade and Wymondley, and another was planned for Weston for the August bank

48   Settlement Ramblers, nd (1940s). GCC 2018.21.20.4

holiday week.[16] By 1934 the members were going further afield; as well as a succession of small camps there had been a holiday camp in Wales.[17] *The Citizen* reported in April 1933 on an indoor camp-fire supper: 'The members sit on the floor around the hearth, in which there is a good fire. The lights of the room are turned out, and then supper is cooked over the fire.'[18] The syllabus for the summer term 1929 noted that 'The Club provides groundsheets, tents and cooking utensils'.[19]

Ramblers Club

It is not clear when this club was formed but there are references from 1946, including details of the outings. The walk on 24 February 1946 was described as Icknield Way (West) and was led by Mr P Titmus. It was not a complete success:

This ramble was spoiled by the fact that it was found impossible to obtain tea at Lilley. Nearly the whole party, however, was equipped with sandwiches etc and we stopped near Deacon Hill for our 'tea'. Mr K Spinks had thought of the idea of bringing the necessary cooking equipment, in order to make tea, but we found to our dismay that no water was available, we all went dry. The 6.30 bus from Lilley was fortunately not overcrowded, but when our party had squeezed in there was standing room only. Arrival home was at 6.55 pm and in spite of the difficulties, I think most people enjoyed the walk.[20]

There were twenty ramblers and the distance was ten miles. Walkers today know how important tea is!

On 8 March 1946 the Student Fellowship Committee reported that the club proposed to affiliate to the National Federation of Rambling Clubs.[21] There was a report of another walk led by Kenneth Spinks on 27 January 1947:

> Tea at the 'Studio Café' Baldock. Half Day. 22 Ramblers. We left the Settlement at 2.35, walking thro' the following places. By road to Norton Fisheries. Path to Radwell. Road to Newnham. Great North Road (2 miles N of Baldock). Arrival at tea place 4.45. Departure from tea place 6.10 walking through, along cinder path, Works Rd. Arrival at Settlement 6.45.[22]

By the AGM on 15 November 1947 the secretary reported that the Rambling Club met regularly and had rediscovered most of north Hertfordshire on their walks. However, less than a year later they were apparently not doing at all well.[23] This appeared to be because of the common problem of not being able to find a secretary, but by 1 December 1950 a Miss Corteen had volunteered her services.[24] Sadly, this situation changed in June 1955 when the disappearance of the club was regretted, with hopes that it might revive.[25] This is a problem still encountered today of course.

Sports clubs

At the AGM on 28 November 1924 James Dudley announced the probable formation of a tennis club and over three years later it was said to have made a good start.[26] In April 1954 it was reported that the club had won the Wilmott Cup in a recent tournament, but had been offered more satisfactory accommodation elsewhere.[27] By October 1956 the new fencing club had also made a good start.[28]

The Art Society

The Art Society was one of the earliest to be formed, being first mentioned on 29 June 1929; a picture exhibition had comprised fifty works by fourteen people and it was hoped to form an Art Club as a result.[29] By May 1953 it was said to be in difficulties but that it might be possible to bring it in as a Settlement Group on a similar basis to the Camera Club.[30] By October 1953 a good beginning had been made by the Art Society as a Settlement Group.[31] It is still in existence, meeting on a Tuesday evening, and there is also a daytime Art Club.

Other societies and groups

There have been a variety of societies and groups over the century. For example, in 1928 a young farmers' club was formed.[32] Others mentioned on different dates include: old-fashioned dances, Esperanto, discussion, travel, portrait,

49   Esperanto Club meeting, 1972. GCC 736.212

mental health, writers' circle, gramophone, recorder, international (for foreign residents and visitors), ciné film and Letchworth Recorded Music Society.[33] Some were lost; in 1987 it was reported that the Bridge Club was too big and would be leaving[34] and in 2004 the Stamp Club decided to amalgamate with the Hitchin one, ending a long association with the Settlement.[35]

Non Settlement groups
By the second half of the twentieth century the number and type of lettings had changed. New ones included the Afternoon Townswomen's Guild, Friends of the Handicapped, Film Society, the local branch of the National Childbirth Trust and a local group of the Royal Society for the Protection of Birds. The warden reported in his 1985/86 annual report that about fifty organisations used the Settlement. One of the most important users today is the Letchworth Arts & Leisure Group (LALG), formed in 1987 and with a huge membership.[36] It has over 100 groups within the umbrella and several of them meet at the Settlement. The current brochure has two pages devoted to Settlement groups; as well as ones already referred to, it features 'Bobbin Along' (making bobbin lace) and HUE (a group of artists working with textiles). There is still a Settlement Table Tennis Group and the Letchworth & Hitchin Chess Club meets there.[37] To quote from a defunct Sunday newspaper, 'all human life is here'.

The Settlement has become an integral part of life in Letchworth Garden City and the use of the building by many groups and societies means that there are few people in the town who are unaware of what it can offer.

Endnotes

1   See <http://settlement-players.co.uk/history/golden-jubilee/>.

2   See <http://settlement-players.co.uk/history/supplement/>.

3   See <https://en.wikipedia.org/wiki/Ben_Greet>.

4   It was refurbished in 2012 and is open to local groups to use; see <https://www.st-francis.herts.sch.uk/facilities.aspx>.

5   It apparently did not survive the first world war, see <https://www.ourwelwyngardencity.org.uk/content/people/c-b-purdom/c_b_purdom>.

6   See <http://www.spads-drama.org.uk/pages/about>.

7   Margaret Bidwell, Hugh's widow, still has a copy of the script.

8   See the Players' website, <settlement-players.co.uk/wppaspec/oc1/cv0/ab82/pt523>.

9   Kryn & Lahy were armament manufacturers founded by Belgian refugees and major employers in the town.

10   Garden City Collection, 2018.21.9.47.

11   Ibid., education box 3

12   Ibid., GCC 2018.21.3.6, *The Citizen*, 13 October 1922.

13   Ibid., LS 7A.

14   Ibid., 2018.21.3.10.

15   Ibid., GCC 2018.21.3.42, *The Citizen*, 11 May 1923.

16   Ibid., LS 7D.

17   Ibid., LS 7I, Council meeting of 17 September 1934.

18   Ibid., 2018.21.15.70.

19   Ibid., 2018.21.9.31.

20   Ibid., 2018.21.30.

21   Ibid., LS 7P.

22   Ibid., 2018.21.30.

23   Ibid., LS 7P.

24   Ibid.

25   Ibid., LS 7R.

26   Ibid., LS 7D.

27   Ibid., LS 7S.

28   Ibid.

29   Ibid., LS 7D.

30   Ibid., LS 7R. The distinction between classes and clubs is dealt with above.

31   Ibid., meeting on 12 October 1953.

32   Ibid., LS 7D.

33   See <https://thefrms.co.uk/affprogs/letch.html>.

34   Garden City Collection, LS 7T, Management Committee meeting, 5 February 1987.

35   Later minutes still at the Settlement, Council meeting, 5 May 2004.

36   See <https://lalg.org.uk/>.

37   See <https://www.letchworthsettlement.org.uk/groups/>.

BIBLIOGRAPHY

Primary sources
Archives of the Settlement now held by the Garden City Collection, reference number 2018.21 and held either at the Garden City Collection [GCC] or in the Nevells Road building itself.

Secondary sources
Armytage, W H G, *Four Hundred Years of English Education*, 2nd edn (Cambridge), 1970

Davies, J S and Freeman, M, 'Education for citizenship: the Joseph Rowntree Charitable Trust and the educational settlement movement', *History of Education*, vol 32, no 3, 2003

Elliott, H and Sanderson, J (co-ordinators), *Letchworth Recollections* (Baldock), 1995

Freeman, M, '"No finer school than a settlement": the development of the educational settlement movement', *History of Education*, vol 31, no 3, 2002

Freeman, M, *The Joseph Rowntree Charitable Trust. A Study in Quaker Philanthropy and Adult Education 1904–1954* (York), 2004

Freeman, M, 'The decline of the adult school movement between the wars', *History of Education*, vol 39, no 4, 2010

Freeman, M, '"An advanced type of democracy"? Governance and politics in adult education, c 1918–1930', *History of Education*, vol 42, no 1, 2013

Ibberson, M, *For joy that we are here. Rural Music Schools 1929–1950* (London), 1977

Kelly, T, *A History of Adult Education in Great Britain* (Liverpool), 1992

Macdonald, K (ed.), *The Conscientious Objector's Wife* (Bath), 2018

Miller, M, *Letchworth. The First Garden City*, 2nd edn (Chichester), 2002

INDEX

LETCHWORTH SETTLEMENT
1920–2020